# THE CHURCH *of the* Perfect Storm

# *More Praise* for
# The Church of the Perfect Storm:

"Let **LEN SWEET** be your guide on a global tour of Christianity's future. Many church leaders find themselves too immersed in local challenges to see impending cultural storms, much less discover what they can do about it. Sweet brings together leading thinkers and futurists to probe where the church is going and how she can remain vibrant and relevant. If you are concerned about impending storms of cultural shifts, relevance, and authenticity, this book will help you not only survive but thrive in the tempest!"

— **Bob Whitesel,** Associate Professor of Graduate Ministry at Indiana Wesleyan University and author of *Inside the Organic Church* (Abingdon Press)

"For those of us who are still trying to steer the ship known as church through the turbulent seas of the twenty-first century, this is a welcomed and prophetic collection of essays filled with insight, inspiration, and hope. This is not a call to stay in a safe harbor ('stay the course') or to batten down the hatches and ride it out ('the way we have always done things'). Rather, in bringing together voices from several seasoned sailors, **LEN SWEET** has provided provocative navigational charts for the future and challenged us all to leave the dock and engage the storm with bold confidence. There is not much smooth sailing through this book, but then those who look for such calm waters have missed the boat anyway. Sail on!"

— **Larry M. Goodpaster,** Resident Bishop, Alabama-West Florida Conference, The United Methodist Church, and author of *There's Power in the Connection* (Abingdon Press)

— Edited by —
Leonard Sweet

# THE CHURCH *of the* Perfect Storm

Abingdon Press
Nashville

THE CHURCH OF THE PERFECT STORM



This book is printed on acid-free paper.

**Library of Congress Cataloging-in-Publication Data**

The church of the perfect storm / Leonard Sweet, editor.
p. cm.
Includes bibliographical references.
ISBN 978-0-687-65089-7 (binding: pbk.: adhesive perfect : alk. paper)
1. Church. 2. Christianity—Forecasting. I. Sweet, Leonard I.

BV600.3.C49 2008
270.8'3—dc22

2007045481



08 09 10 11 12 13 14 15 16 17—10 9 8 7 6 5 4 3 2 1

MANUFACTURED IN THE UNITED STATES OF AMERICA

To

John David Sweet

*the best wave-rider in the world*

**Acknowledgments** . . . . . . . . . . . . . . . . . . . . . . . . . . . . **ix**

**Introduction:** Born in a Storm . . . . . . . . . . . . . . . . . . . . . . . . **xi**
LEONARD SWEET (United States)

**Chapter 1:** Outstorming Christianity's Perfect Storm . . . . . **1**
LEONARD SWEET (United States)

**Chapter 2:** Man Overboard! . . . . . . . . . . . . . . . . . . . . . . . . **37**
GREG GLATZ (Canada)

**Chapter 3:** In Sync with Jesus and the First Perfect Stormers . . . . . . . . . . . . . . . . . . . . . . . . . . . . **42**
STEPHAN JOUBERT (South Africa)

**Chapter 4:** Seasoned Sailors . . . . . . . . . . . . . . . . . . . . . . . . **52**
ALAN JAMIESON (New Zealand)

**Chapter 5:** Exposing Our Murky Motives . . . . . . . . . . . . **62**
DRIES LOMBAARD (South Africa)

**Chapter 6:** Reorienting the Church of the Twenty-first Century . . . . . . . . . . . . . . . . . . . . .**72**
YOUNGLAE KIM (South Korea)

**Chapter 7:** The Perfect Storm as a Paradigmic Theory . .**82**
EARL J. PIERCE (United States)

**Chapter 8:** Mid-storm Equations for the Emerging Church . . . . . . . . . . . . . . . . . . . . . . . .**89**
BILL EASUM (United States)

**Chapter 9:** The Tides Are Turning . . . . . . . . . . . . . . . . . .**99**
MICHAEL BLEWETT (United States)

**Chapter 10:** The Relationships of Winds and Waves . .**109**
MARK BATTERSON (United States)

**Chapter 11:** Between Spirit and Culture . . . . . . . . . . . . .**119**
THOMAS G. BANDY (Canada)

**Chapter 12:** Celestial Storms: Dreaming of Novae . . . .**139**
PETER J. WALKER (United States)

**Chapter 13:** Manual and Chart Notes for Stormy Seas **144**
LEONARD SWEET (United States)

**List of Contributors** . . . . . . . . . . . . . . . . . . . . . . . . . . . . . .**161**

**Notes** . . . . . . . . . . . . . . . . . . . . . . . . . . . . . . . . . . . . . . .**165**

# ACKNOWLEDGMENTS

Anthologies are strange beasts. You might call them the platypuses of the publishing world: mammals that live in the water but lay eggs and nurse, or in the language of the book trade, composite beings that mix and match a variety of creatures and features.

Although the creature you hold in your hand is no different in its ungainly appearance than other anthologies, certain people helped to make this one do more than prove (as the platypus is said to do) that God has a sense of humor.

My doctoral students from George Fox University commented on this manuscript and made numerous suggestions for improvements. From LEC (Leadership in the Emerging Culture) cohorts: James Armstrong, Christopher Arney, Stephen Campbell, Rick Chromey, Alan Ehler, Mark B. Hale, Joey Harlow, (Brad) Donald Bradley Henson, David McDonald, Ted Moeller, Tim Ozment, Jerry W. Payne, Eddie Rester, Evangeline Willms Thiessen, John Tittle, Denis Bell, Bryan Benjamin, Henry Berg, Chuck Coward, John Frank, Greg Glatz, Randy Groves, Kerry McRoberts, Quintin Moore, Patrick Murunga, Lars Rood, Brian Ross, Christine Roush, Jeffrey Tacklind, Fourie van den Berg, and Jacob Youmans.

A very special thanks to colleague Terry O'Casey, who gave the manuscript the closest of critical readings. Terry doesn't approach the Bible as docudrama, but I have learned from him to experience more deeply the drama and even melodrama of the Scriptures. Greg Glatz did a masterful job of making editable, and thus edible, an assortment of essays, some of which were written in a second language. His encouragement that this piece of subject matter was worth biting off kept me going during the easy times and the hard.

Henry James once remarked that, in art, the desire to do good often interfered with the ability to do well. My biggest hope is that *The Church of the Perfect Storm* gives off some sense of art in the first place. If so, it is due in no small measure to the efforts of Betty O'Brien, my research assistant. It is because of her friendship and spirit that I have been able to "take courage" and make these words my own. They were written by William Cowper (1731–1800) but immediately spread throughout Christianity, becoming some of the favorite words of Cardinal John Henry Newman's ministry:

*Ye fearful saints fresh courage take,*
*The clouds ye so much dread*
*Are big with mercy and shall break*
*In blessings on your head.*

*Judge not the Lord by feeble sense,*
*But trust him for his grace;*
*Behind a frowning providence*
*He hides a smiling face.*[1]

LEONARD SWEET
Orcas Island
July 4, 2007

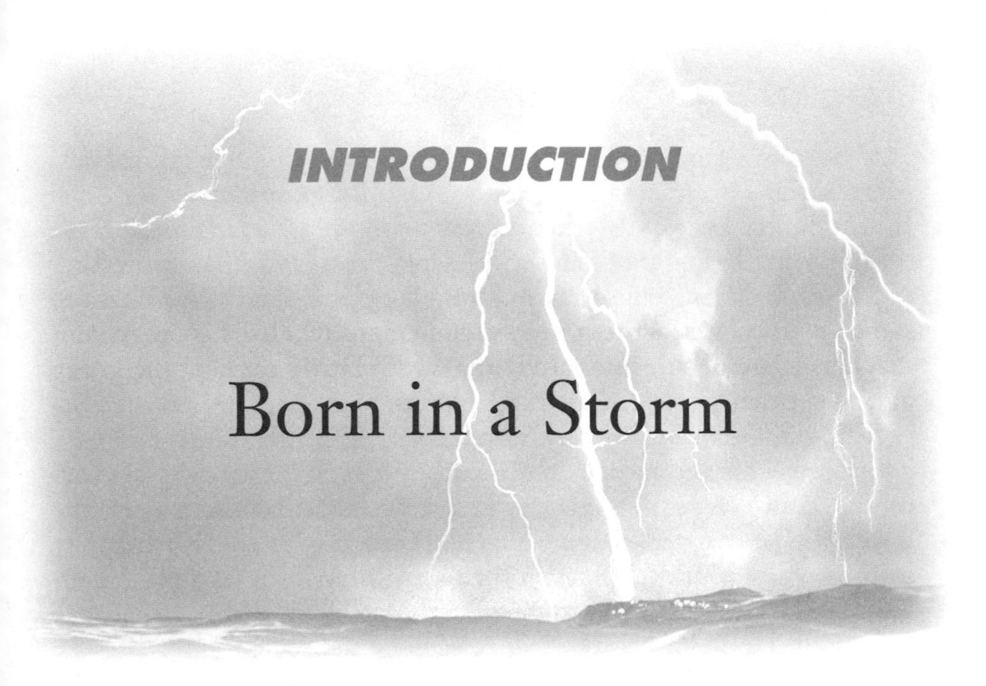

# INTRODUCTION

# Born in a Storm

A Scarface song has lyrics that are taken from an expression of the black church. After reminding us that we're either heading into a storm, in a storm now, or just leaving one, the song tells us, "yeah think about it."[1]

This book is an attempt to get the church to "think about it." We invited thinkers from around the world, some established, some emerging, to get their wettest in an attempt to get the church thinking and talking about what it might mean that you and I were born in a storm—not just any storm, but arguably Christianity's first perfect storm.

Certain cultures make a big deal of children who were born in a storm. They give them special names, surround them with special responsibilities, or raise them with special training. Of course, if each one of us is either leaving a storm, heading into a storm, or in the midst of a storm, that means that every person who has ever lived has been born in a storm. But some have been born when parents were living all three storms (in/out/midst) at once.

***A Storm Like No Other:*** Lifestorms are one thing to think about. Culturestorms are another. This collection of essays explores the possibility that being born in a storm now has an uncommon, unique meaning: Christians are now headed into one of the greatest culturestorms ever. We are calling it the church of the perfect storm.

When did we enter this perfect culturestorm? Some historical cutoffs are neat and clean; others are iffy and fuzzy. For example, 1967 was the semiofficial cutoff date for addressing God as *Thou* and *you* in the official liturgiography of English.[2] As an adolescent, I can remember making that transition and sharing the struggle of those who refused to change their divine address (a powerful essay lobbying for the continued use of *Thou* by the pastor of Riverside Church, Ernest T. Campbell, almost persuaded me off the you path). Other historical transitions, like the one under discussion in this book, are not nearly so clear. In fact, you will see that the authors in this anthology exhibit a variety of views on the nature of this transition as well as on its periodization.

***Storm Warnings:*** No doubt this book creaks more heavily than the ship it's about. But the essays in this born-in-a-storm warning are offered in the spirit of the words spoken to a storm-tossed Jeremiah, the Eeyore of the Bible, when he was rejected and dejected:

> If you have raced with people on foot
> and they have worn you out,
> how can you compete with horses?
> If you stumble in safe country,
> how will you manage in the thickets by the Jordan?[3]

In other words, "Cheer up, Jeremiah, there's worse to come."

Cheer up, brothers and sisters of the church of the perfect storm, it's gonna get worse.

Remember the old saw about pessimists and optimists: pessimists believe things could not get worse; optimists know they could.

Cheer up! Things will get worse.

And again I say, "cheer up!"

Or as Jesus himself warned his disciples, "In the world you will have tribulation [storms]." This is not a counsel of despair, but a fact of life. Storms and problems are not separate from the whole-life that Jesus promised his disciples in John 10:10. They are a part of it, even contained within it.

Jesus continues: "But be of good cheer [take courage], I have overcome the world."[4]

*You have put gladness in my heart,*
*More than in the season that their grain and wine increased.*

PSALM 4:7 NKJV[5]

The "good cheer" and "courage" for those born in a storm are based not on facts, but on faith. The facts of life are frightening. But our future is secure in the God who "plants his footsteps in the sea, / And rides upon the storm."[6]

## CHAPTER ONE

# Outstorming Christianity's Perfect Storm

LEONARD SWEET *(United States)*

*For I am the LORD your God,*
*who churns up the sea so that its waves roar—*
*the LORD Almighty is his name.*
*Isaiah 51:15 NIV*

There is a reason you are so tired.

There is a reason your church is woozy from the worship wars.

There is a reason society is pining for simpler, safer times.

There is a reason people are cranky, dispirited, and suffering from an acute case of holy halitosis or unholy hypothermia.

There is a reason theologians seem to be commentators on a game that no one is playing.

There is a reason the Christian church has lost pride in itself or in what it does.

There is a reason for the cultural dooms and glooms, all the vertigo and violence.

There is a reason that every time you read the newspaper, you want to pray a prayer seemingly written just for this world of ours: "Lord, have mercy."

There is a reason Armageddon is in the air.

There is a reason hysteria, meanness, and boredom seem to be the prevailing Christian temper.

There is a reason there are now 2,088 country music stations in the United States, more than any other single radio format.

There is a reason that two recent number one country-and-western hits were Rascal Flatts's "Mayberry" and Tim McGraw's "Back When":

> I miss Mayberry . . .
> Where everything is black and white[1]

and

> I like the old and outdated
> Way of life.[2]

The reason is more than the fact that the world seems out of control. Or that in my lifetime we have gone from *Pride and Prejudice* to *The Princess Diaries*, from *Leave It to Beaver* to *Beavis and Butt-Head*, from *Queen for a Day* to *Desperate Housewives*, from doo-wop to bebop to hip-hop. Or that in these dawning days of the twenty-first century the biblical story is now so unfamiliar that the leading interfaith journal can identify the phrase "be in the world but not of it," not as a quote from Jesus but as an old "Sufi saying."[3]

The reason is this: we're entering the perfect storm.[4]

*His way is in whirlwind and storm,*
*and the clouds are the dust of his feet.*

NAHUM 1:3 NIV

***Past storms:*** To be sure, this is not the first time Christians have had to pass through culturestorms that have been more than ripples on the surface of Christianity. To paraphrase Job, there is no end of storms. The church is born to storms, surely as waves crash the shore.[5] Saint Basil once compared the church after the Council of Nicea with a naval battle in the darkness of a storm.[6] Clipper ships like the *Cutty Sark* were once known as "Gothic cathedrals" at sail. Here are some examples of when and where the clipper ship of Christianity has found itself between the devil and the deep blue sea:

1. Jesus was born in the midst of a storm, a time of state-sponsored terror (the terrorist's name was Herod).

2. In the second century, Christians transitioned from thinking of themselves as a branch of Judaism and began viewing themselves as a unique movement, to the horror of the Judaizers.

3. When the church was in the midst of the last days of Roman North Africa as Rome fell in A.D. 410 to the barbarian Visigoths, Augustine of Hippo spent ten years writing a manual on how to get through this storm. This manual was called *The City of God*.[7]

4. When the church was facing an alien philosophical system called Aristotelianism, a brilliant intellect named Thomas Aquinas studied this amazing body of knowledge for an entire lifetime. He wrote a book, *Summa Theologiae*, that both integrated and critiqued this vast body of pagan insight.

5. When the church confronted a new technology called the printing press that proposed new delivery systems for learning and faith formation, Martin Luther, John Calvin, and others led a Protestant Reformation that embraced the new technology and, in so doing, shook the very foundations of Christian tradition.

*The dogmas of the quiet past are inadequate to the stormy present.*

ABRAHAM LINCOLN[8]

In these first decades of the twenty-first century, there are storm clouds not just on the horizon, but overhead. This is more than simply making heavy weather about the weather. An unblinking conversation with history reveals that the transformations taking place during the current culturestorms are without precedent in Christian history. Three storm-makers, all global storms, all Category 5 storms, all overlapping, mutually reinforcing, multiple storms, have created collectively what might be called the perfect storm.[9]

First is the tsunami known as postmodernity.[10] Second is the big hurricane, or more precisely an epidemic of related hurricanes, called post-Christendom. The third is a global warming I am calling post-scale. Any one of these storms could smash the clipper ship of Christianity to pieces. Each one of these storms requires huge adjustments. All three together constitute what can perhaps best be described as the perfect storm. No compass has ever been invented for the perfect storm.

***The Day After the Day After:*** Is this the end of Christianity as we know it?[11] The storm is taking Christianity where no Christian has gone before. History hangs too heavily at this point in time for the church not to feel a new, accelerated urgency as it faces its terrible moment in history. If the church is not watchful and wakeful, it will find itself pirated by the cultural moment, just as it was by fascism, just as it was by Nazism.

*We are all faced with a series of great opportunities brilliantly disguised as insoluble problems.*

JOHN GARDNER[12]

The perfect storm does not set this time of history in a minor key. That is why every place today seems to be in the process of both being born and dying. The Perfect Storm is much more than a historical marker (*chronos* time). It is a historical opportunity (*kairos* time). These are some of the most exciting, extraordinary, *kairo*tic days the church has ever experienced. *Kairos* time summons leaders who will leave the comfortable and conventional. *Kairos* time summons leaders who will not try to reverse history or make time flow backwards. The best you cheat the clock is only one hour, which we do each spring and fall. *Kairos* time summons men and women of faith, in Søren Kierkegaard's magnificent phrase, who will "remain out upon the deep, over seventy thousand fathoms of water, still preserving my faith."[13]

The call is greater than ever before, but it is not for the faint of heart. But then, whoever said it was supposed to be easy? Jesus warned us to sit down and "consider the cost" before we decide to follow him.[14]

In both the book and the movie *The Perfect Storm*, there was one reason to go out into the storm and risk being lost at sea: to make the ultimate catch. I would argue that the perfect storm offers the church its greatest chance to become the "Ultimate Church" and make the ultimate catch for the gospel. Navigate this sea change, cross this raging "Red Sea,"[15] and we will find a promised land of new beginnings and a new church on the other side. What is certain is that the future will be far better for the church than the past. What is also certain is that many churches will be left behind, smash on the shoals of status-quoism, or sink into oblivion.

Storms prune and purify. They tear down all that is not tied down and lasting. They enforce the rule of persevere or perish.[16] It behooves us to make the most of our storms, especially this perfect storm. For in the words of British Methodist Colin Morris, "God wills a new creation which may be a gift from beyond history, the kingdom of heaven, but which is made up of elements from every era in history that have withstood the shaking, gone through the refiner's fire and had the dross burned off them."[17]

When everyone and everything is spinning and whirling in the wind, Christians go out to meet the storm. Christians embrace the wind.

And pass out kites.

*The natural flights of the human mind are not from pleasure to pleasure, but from hope to hope.*

SAMUEL JOHNSON[18]

## Category 5 Cultural Storm: The Tsunami of Postmodernity

*We have learned a new word—tsunami—*
*which you already knew, Lord,*
*for you created this world*
*in all its beauty and terror.*
*Hallowed be your name.*

. . . .

*And may we all resolve*
*to revere this fragile earth rather than abuse it,*
*to enable developing nations rather than indebt them,*
*and to claim your presence*
*rather than fear your absence*
*at the heart of every storm.*

A PRAYER WRITTEN BY JOHN BELL OF THE IONA COMMUNITY FOR THE BBC SPECIAL "SONGS OF PRAISE VIGIL" AFTER THE 2005 TSUNAMI[19]

Nobody woke up one morning and said:

I've got a wonderful feeling; tsunami is coming my way.[20]

But that is exactly what has happened in many of our lifetimes. A tsunami called postmodernity has inundated planet Earth, not just one privileged part of the planet, the whole planet. The notion that postmodernity is limited to Western, Anglo cultures is belied by two stories:

1. In February of 2006, seventy-four people died in the Philippines. They were in a waiting crowd of over thirty thousand people that stampeded to get inside the PhilSports Arena (in the Pasig suburb outside Manila) for a reality TV game show *Wowowee* where the grand prize was one million pesos ($19,300).[21]

2. In early 2007 I received an e-mail from a friend in Slovakia. His grandmother lives in a ramshackle house that has no indoor plumbing but does have broadband access to the Internet.

For pomo-phobes, postmodernity means just about anything you want it to mean, as long as it is objectionable. But no one can escape the fact that the twenty-first century is operating off of very different assumptions and energies than characterized the previous couple of centuries. Anyone want to argue that our kids are living in an entirely different thought world than the one we grew up in, and that these two worlds often do not speak to each other? Anyone born after 1964 want to argue that our kids have brains wired differently from ours? Any educator want to defend the big jug/little mug learning plan, memorialized in a bit of adolescent doggerel:

> Cram it in, jam it in;
> People's heads are hollow.
> Take it in, pour it in;
> There is more to follow.[22]

The human brain works differently now than it used to.

The people of Peoria, Illinois, proved it over a century ago. It was the afternoon of 16 October 1854. An obscure former one-term congressman named Abraham Lincoln debated the well-known Democratic Senator Stephen Douglas. The issue was the Kansas-Nebraska Act, which was passed a couple of months earlier and whose primary author was Senator Douglas. Lincoln made public his bill of complaints against this bill and outlined his opposition to the extension of slavery into Kansas made possible by this bill.

This debate was a trial run for the more famous Lincoln-Douglas debates of 1858.

Douglas kicked things off at 2:00 P.M. He mesmerized the Peoria crowd for three straight hours.

When Lincoln rose to speak, he surprised his audience by dismissing them. "I'm hungry," he told his listeners. "Take a break, get something to eat, and come back in an hour." Since he promised not to take any less time than his esteemed colleague, and assured Douglas that he would have sufficient time for rebuttal, Lincoln warned everyone that at least another four hours of listening awaited them.

At 7:00 P.M. sharp, a miracle took place. The Peorians came back. They went home, but most amazing of all, they came back for another four hours.[23] The only person in recent memory who could command the attention of a crowd for seven hours is Fidel Castro, and even then it wasn't exactly a voluntary attention.

It is almost as if the church willfully will not hear the news: the world has moved on.

We may not know what this new world is, but we know what it isn't. In the words of the late philosopher Stanley Grenz, "postmodernism refers to an intellectual mood and an array of cultural expressions that call into question the ideals, principles, and values that lay at the heart of the modern mind-set."[24] The modern project has ended. "Postmodernity" is the name given to this fragmentary, digital, dizzying world of kaleidoscopic changes, a world where everything often comes to nothing. Or in the words of one theological dictionary, postmodern is the void between the lost and the not yet comprehended: "Postmodern is the name given to this space between what was and what is yet to be."[25]

Some mourn modernity's passing (modernists). Others never liked modernism in the first place (premoderns/traditionalists). Some celebrate modernism's demise, but still define themselves in terms of modernity (call these the neo-avant-garde[26] who still pursue the new but a different and often recycled new from the modern). The relation between premodern, modern, and postmodern is not sequential, but simultaneous. The tsunami of postmodernity did not wash away all outcroppings of premodern or modern. If it had, we would need to rebuild them. There are premodern parts of me, and modern parts of me, and postmodern parts of me. But the primary cultural formation out of which we must operate is now postmodern.

*The premodern period was characterized by faith in God and knowledge based on authoritative tradition. . . . In the modern paradigm, the emphasis was changed from faith in God to human reasoning. . . . In the postmodern period . . . we are moving away from reason by the autonomous self and moving toward relationship in community.*

JIMMY LONG[27]

***Premoderns:*** Premodern people trusted authoritative texts that were mediated by trusted authority figures (king, bishop, Roman hierarchy). Critical reasoning or empirical experimentation were foreign concepts, as was the ideal of freedom, whether freedom to choose your spouse, your career, your location, not to mention freedom of speech, press, assembly, or freedom of conscience. Notions of the self revolved around an innate and inherited human nature, which remained the same for everyone.[28]

In premodern worship, the high point was the Eucharist, when God meets humans in the wine and bread. A lot else happened in worship, but this was the moment everyone waited for, the moment so powerful that some people fainted, the *hoc est corpus meum* (hocus pocus) moment.

***Moderns:*** The modern makeover was accomplished by Descartes, Locke, Galileo, and Guttenberg. They made the world over and birthed a new kind of reality by using certain drivers: doubt, the rhetoric of reason, and natural rights theory. The word *cogito* was not original to Descartes (Augustine was very high on *cogito* centuries before). But Descartes's *cogito ergo sum* is seen as the starting point of Enlightenment culture, where people trusted in individual or collective reason as the ultimate authority and denigrated emotion and intuition.[29]

With trust in the power of reason came the doctrine of progress. Where do you think we get the notion that democracy and free markets are preordained to spread around the globe? The doctrine of progress and modernism go hand in hand. Notions of reason replaced premodern notions of human nature when it came to understandings of the self, and it was assumed that human nature is rational. Premodern bowing before God gave way to modern bowing before Me.[30]

Modernity was when religion and art took leave of one another.

Modernity was when religion and the apocalyptic took leave of one another.[31]

Modernity was when organized religion and the nation-state took to bed with one another, and civil religion was born.[32]

*Nothing is more foreign to us than the state. One state we know, of which all are citizens.*

THIRD-CENTURY THEOLOGIAN TERTULLIAN[33]

But even at the height of modernity, some registered doubt about doubt. Here is philosopher David Hume, obsessed with how his logic and reason have both the power to do good and the power to totally wreck people's lives, imagining himself as "a kind of monster who had infected his fellow thinkers with crushing doubts:"

> I dine, I play a game of back-gammon, I converse, and am merry with my friends; and when after three or four hour's amusement, I wou'd return to these speculations, they appear so cold, and strain'd, and ridiculous, that I cannot find in my heart to enter into them any further. Here then I find myself absolutely and necessarily determin'd to live, and talk, and act like other people in the common affairs of life. . . . But . . . I still feel such remains of my former disposition, that I am ready to throw all my books and papers into the fire, and resolve never more to renounce the pleasure of life for the sake of reasoning and philosophy. . . . If I must be a fool, as all those who reason or believe any thing certainly are, my follies shall at least be natural and agreeable.[34]

In modern worship, the high point was the sermon. The notion of bread becoming flesh and wine becoming blood sounds superstitious, irrational, and unscientific. What everyone waited for was the elevation, not of a host but of a homily, now a lecture, a new insight or knowledge that would be passed out by the professionals to the people. Christianity so sold out to modernity that, as Reinhold Niebuhr noted back in the 1930s, the two became almost indistinguishable.

*Protestant Christianity in America is, unfortunately, unduly dependent upon the very culture of modernity, the disintegration of which would offer a more independent religion a unique opportunity.*

REINHOLD NIEBUHR[35]

***Postmoderns:*** Postmoderns want to know: Why does there have to be a reason for everything? There is a loss of confidence in *both* pre-modern authority figures and modern reason. Postmoderns no longer trust the human powers of reasoning to solve everything. In fact, one author describes postmodernity as "a certain loss of faith—faith in the power of reason to resolve differences and deliver solutions—and a consequent loss of hope—hope in progress based on human knowledge."[36] For postmoderns it is less "Aha! Now I get it. I've figured it out" and more "Aha! Now I feel it. I've experienced exactly what you're talking about."

Postmoderns feel badly burned: badly burned by science, badly burned by modernists, badly burned by the church, badly burned by philosophy, and so on. Reason didn't usher in the "kingdom of God," much less the "kingdom of man."[37] If anything, reason ushered in the kingdom of Stalin, Hitler, and Mao. Zygmunt Bauman argues that the Holocaust and its camps were some of modernity's highest expressions of Enlightenment thinking, and the supreme example of the Enlightenment project.[38]

Postmoderns tend to be ironical and cynical. They continually collapse ideals and dreams into power relations. Truth is power. The advantage of being a "reasonable Creature," proto-pomo Benjamin Franklin observed, is that you can find a reason for whatever you want to do.[39] Constantine was the first Christian emperor. He proposed to build a triad of churches in Constantinople, his new capital: one would be dedicated to holy peace (Hagia Eirene—more premodern), one dedicated to holy wisdom (Hagia Sophia—more modern); and one dedicated to holy power. He built the first two. He failed to construct the third, the one to holy power. Postmoderns are doing that for him.

Not that postmoderns reject all understandings of truth. They allow for certain kinds of truth. Just not absolute truth that applies equally to all cultures. Philosopher Richard Rorty smiles as he says this: "Truth is what your contemporaries will let you get away with."[40] We are living in an age when truth, as in the days of Isaiah the prophet, "has stumbled in the streets" and is "nowhere to be found."[41] Nietzsche was wrong. God is not dead. For postmoderns, God is not in a coffin, but in a cabinet of curiosities.

*If we are not tasting the fullness of the now,*
*we will play the games of power to fill the emptiness.*

RICHARD ROHR[42]

To "follow your bliss" is to follow your truth. But postmoderns believe that truth is found in relationship, that through dialogue and discussion truths are discovered. The advertising world has moved from "telling and selling" to "building relationships," which includes word of mouth but more importantly features social networking. To postmoderns, all voices are equal, and amateurs are as much entitled to schooling experts as professionals may feel they are to school the uneducated. The priesthood of the bridge—the elite clergy of religion and science—is being replaced by the priesthood of all on deck.

As symbolized by replacing the codex with the scroll (via computer mouse), a technological step backwards, postmoderns are more premodern than modern. There is nothing more universally postmodern than purveyors of ancient identities. This is why Princess Diana ("Shy Di") was such a global sensation, combining into one visage premodern royalty with postmodern celebrity. Postmoderns may be scientifically more sophisticated than ever before, but they are as liable as anyone else in history to believe in ghosts or aliens or interdimensional visitations or macrobiotic diets. In fact, in terms of spiritual obsessions, the United States is closer to Turkey, India, or Egypt than to Sweden, Germany, or the United Kingdom. Canada is a country where 70 percent say they are Christian. And twice as many Canadians read their horoscopes for personal guidance as read their Bibles.

*Today dogmatisms feed and flourish on the desecrated corpse of reason. Astrology, prophecy, homeopathy, Feng shui, conspiracy theories, flying saucers, voodoo, crystal balls, miracle-working angel visits, alien abductions, management nostrums, and a thousand other cults dominate people's minds, often with official backing.*

PHILOSOPHER AND COGNITIVE SCIENTIST JERRY A. FODOR[43]

The postmodern self is socially constructed. There is no essence to human nature. Besides, postmoderns look not to find what's common (that's premodern and modern) but what's different and unique. Everything is flux and fluid. The late Jean Baudrillard notoriously defined the postmodern age in terms of the ascendancy of simulacra over the "desert of the real."[44] Solid ground is as much a myth as the solid surface of the Earth is a myth. When you know what's going on beneath the earth, under your feet, you realize how ungrounded we all are. Just ask any seismologist, who will talk to you about the molten core, fault lines, and the liquidity of rocks. The continents travel on a mobile sea floor. Hence the popularity of images of sea or aqua and journeying as the two dominant metaphors for postmodernity.[45] When the sea floors move, the tsunami appears.

*I'm constantly amazed at how threatened some people are by Christianity.*

KEVIN WILSON[46]

## Category 5 Religious Storm: The Hurricane of Post-Christendom

In Brussels, over 50 percent of the babies born are Muslim. In England, there are now more practicing Muslims than practicing Anglicans. Islam has become the largest European religion (*not* Catholicism). Pope John Paul II could fill any stadium in the world, but his papacy couldn't fill one church in Europe.

Do you know how you can tell a European Catholic is paranoid?

They think someone's sitting behind them in worship.

In Europe, Christians are almost an endangered species. At the same time that Christianity is dying the West, Christianity is surging in the East and in the South. The statistical center of Christianity today is in Timbuktu, Mali. The language of Christianity today is Spanish; the color of Christianity today is not white but brown; there are more Christian churches in India today than in the United States.[47] By 2025, two-thirds of Christians will live in Latin America, Africa, and Asia.

The West is deconstructing, and Christianity is dying in the West.[48] These two not unrelated phenomenon have created a post-Christendom culture.[49]

When Constantine adopted Christianity as the state religion in the early fourth century, the Christian story was central to how Western culture saw itself and to the shaping of its social institutions. This cozy relationship between church and state created a Christendom culture where church and culture washed each other's hands.

In post-Christendom culture, the culture has washed its hands of the church.[50] Ralph Waldo Emerson once said that Christianity was not so much "proclaimed" as it was "plowed" into Western history.[51]

Well, that plowing is over, and the evidence of that plowing is getting less and less.

*In that ago when being was believing*

W. H. AUDEN[52]

Even those who weren't Christian, lived out of a Christendom discourse and picked up the soundtrack. Take an extreme example: Mickey Mouse. Could a non-Christian culture have produced a hero like Mickey Mouse? Even though Walt Disney was afraid of mice, he seemed to get the Christian notion that out of the least comes the greatest. This is what so mystified the Nazis, in one example of their Disney bashing:

> Mickey Mouse is the most miserable ideal ever revealed. . . . Healthy emotions tell every independent young man and every honorable youth that the dirty and filth-covered vermin, the greatest bacteria carrier in the animal kingdom, cannot be the ideal type of animal![53]

Christianity is no longer the cement that holds society together. It is no longer the common backdrop or mortar of the culture. And even where it's still present, it's only there as a chipped and faded veneer that is vanishing rapidly. Callum Brown, in his book *The Death of Christian Britain* (2006), shakes his head in amazement at how quickly this happened: "It took several centuries to convert Britain to Christianity, but it has taken less than forty years for the country to forsake it."[54] Just like each one of us is sculpted by the soundtrack of our teen years and obsessed with that soundtrack for the rest of our days, Western culture has been sculpted by the soundtrack of Christianity. But that soundtrack today is missing. Those of us who still hear it can sing its melodies to our heart's content. But the emerging culture looks on us like we look at those who sing to a soundtrack only they can hear: the lips are moving, and notes are being hit, but the soundtrack isn't playing; and at best we feel pity and embarrassment for the singer.

*We will, unless there is a turn in the tide, be a Church that gradually disappears from the land.*

ANGLICAN BISHOP OF MANCHESTER, NIGEL MCCULLOCH[55]

The shift from a Christendom culture to a post-Christendom culture is the difference between experiencing a sacred art work in a church with the gathered people of God, and looking at a sacred painting in a museum. The former experience is gone forever. In the words of Stuart Murray, post-Christendom culture is "a culture in which central features of the Christian story are unknown and churches are alien institutions whose rhythms do not normally impinge on most members of society."[56]

One of my favorite artists, Edward Knippers, tells of his frustration at painting Christian themes in a culture with little Christian memory or rhythms:

> A middle-aged woman came to my studio and was standing in front of my *Stoning of Stephen*. I told her the title. She seemed intrigued by it but looked at me with no registration at all. I thought she hadn't heard me so I repeated the title and added, 'That is an account in the Bible.' She said 'Oh yes, the Bible. Is that Old or New Testament?' I said it is New Testament, the first Christian martyr. Then she said, 'Now I know why you used so much blue. That is the color I see when I meditate.' I said, 'No, that's sky.' That is indicative of the society in which we live.[57]

More people now recognize the golden arches than the cross or the crescent. In my lifetime it's now a holiday season, not a Christmas season; it's now a holiday tree, not a Christmas tree. After Thanksgiving every year, Starbucks sells two blends that are exactly the same but with two different names: Christmas blend and Holiday blend. Nicholas Lash, a theologian at the University of Cambridge, reveals the following in a recent book: "A few years ago, a survey was conducted amongst seventeen year olds in the Czech Republic. Only one percent of those interviewed were skinheads, but eight percent knew what skinheads were about. Only fifteen percent said that they were Christians. Readers presuming that to be bad news should brace themselves for worse: the percentage of those interviewed who knew what Christianity was about was—fifteen!"[58]

It is no longer permitted at town council meetings or football games to end a prayer with "in the name of Jesus." How different this is from the world in which I was born—a world of blue laws, a world where stores were closed on Good Friday from noon to 3:00 P.M., a world where red-letter Christians trusted all the Bible but treated the red letters as the first among equals. The rhythms of sacred time, once canonized in the calendar as Yom Kippur or Lent, have now been cleansed as spring break. In USAmerica, a Jew can be a Jew, a Buddhist can be a Buddhist, a Muslim can be a Muslim, but let a Christian be a Christian and see what animosity breaks forth.

*Young people are now more likely to have heard of feng shui, chi and yoga than the Trinity, the Ascension and the Resurrection. In everyday discourse Christian concepts have become rare.*

BRITISH SOCIOLOGIST LINDA WOODHEAD[59]

In a Christendom culture, what we wanted in a church was a place to baptize our children and a place to be buried by our children.

In post-Christendom culture, the church is a scary place, the Bible is a book sometimes seen in a hotel room drawer, and the crucifixion showcases "some dead man on a stick."[60] Stuart Murray, in one of his "snapshots of post-Christendom," tells of a London teenager who hears the Christmas story for the first time. "His teacher tells it well and he is fascinated by this amazing story. Risking his friends' mockery, after the lesson he thanks her for the story. One thing had disturbed him, so he asks: 'Why did they give the baby a swear word for his name?' "[61]

My first theological act was childhood rewriting of a bedtime prayer. In what seems a universe away, I had been taught never to climb under the covers before kneeling by my bed and saying this prayer:

> Now I lay me down to sleep,
> I pray thee Lord my soul to keep,
> If I should die before I wake,
> I pray thee Lord my soul to take.

A parent teaching that prayer to a child today would be open to child endangerment charges. Even as a child I felt it was somewhat harsh, so I dared my first theological critique, and emended the prayer to say "If thou should'st come before I wake, I pray thee Lord my body to take." Kids today have graduated from knowing bedtime prayers to knowing about Clinton's infidelities, Madonna and Brittney's kiss, and a new set of meaning to the images of pup tents and cowboys. Kids today also grow up with children's literature that mocks Christianity.[62]

People aren't hearing us. And those who are hearing us don't like what they're hearing. Post-Christian increasingly blends into anti-Christian. Of course, there has always been an anti-Christian element in USAmerican history. It was even present at our nation's founding. Thomas Jefferson believed that "Christianity is the most perverted system that ever shone on man." Benjamin Franklin contended that "lighthouses are more useful than churches." James Madison observed that the "fruits of Christianity" are "pride and indolence in the clergy" and "ignorance and servility in the laity."[63]

Postmodern culture doesn't really like fish people (named after those fish-shaped bumper stickers): it deems fish people to be clammy, slimy, and smelly. For postmoderns, their default position is that religion is bad for you; spirituality may be good, but religion is bad. Howard Stern, the highest paid entertainer in history, has a sidekick named Robin. In response to one of Pat Robertson's political commentaries, she announced: "I'm moving to Canada. I don't want to live in a Christian nation." Christianity has yet to get used to a level playing field between it and other faith communities much less people like Robin with no religious community at all.

In Christendom culture, going to church is seen to make you a better person. In post-Christendom culture, going to church makes you a more boring, mean, and judgmental person. After 9/11, the days are gone when religion is seen as "a good thing." Both the Koran and the Bible are seen as the deadliest texts on the planet.

Christianity is seen as something that makes a person less human, more faithless, hopeless, and loveless. Most postmoderns don't fret over whether Christianity can get you to heaven; they want to know will it make you a better person. What Christians can't seem to understand is that postmoderns deem people who believe in moral absolutes as morally inferior and more prone to evil than those who are moral relativists.[64] Some argue, with good cause, that the term *Christian* is now polluted beyond recognition.

*And with the guts of the last priest*
*Let's shake the neck of the last king.*

ENLIGHTENMENT *PHILISOPHE* DENIS DIDEROT[65]

There have always been currents of anti-Christian sentiment circulating in academic and literary circles. When T. S. Eliot became an Anglican (that is, Anglo-Catholic), Virginia Woolf derided his decision: he "may be called dead to us from this day forward . . . I mean, there's something obscene in a living person sitting by the fire and believing in God."[66] Novelist William Empson was a Christian-baiter and hater.[67] Gore Vidal dismissively calls Christ-followers "Christers."[68] Noel Annan tells the story of when he was provost at King's College. He tried to convince the biologist and DNA-discoverer Francis Crick to apply for a fellowship, but Crick refused. His reason was that he could not join any group that had a chapel: to associate his name with religion would compromise with falsehood and be a pact with the devil.[69]

But the anti-Christian sentiment of a post-Christendom culture is of a very different order. People opposed to Christianity in a Christendom culture were still arguing *with* Christianity. Post-Christendom people simply argue *against* Christianity. I shall never forget a 2005 radio interview and call-in show on CBC Radio out of Calgary, Alberta.

The amount of venom and vitriol that came my way over the radio was severe: "I hate Christians," "Christians are the worst people in the world," and "the church is the last place I'd go to deal with my spirituality." But of all the calls I received the last caller was the one I'll never forget. He admitted to being "over sixty." Then he continued: "I used to be a Christian. But after a lifetime of listening to Christians cutting this person down, and hating that kind of person, I became an atheist. Do you hear me, Dr. Sweet? I became an atheist because of Christians."

With the almost simultaneous publication of four books, the year 2006 marked the rise of an aggressive atheism that positioned itself almost as much against Christianity as in favor of agnosticism/atheism.[70] The four books are Sam Harris's *The End of Faith* (which quickly sold more than one-quarter million copies), Richard Dawkins's *The God Delusion*, Daniel C. Dennett's *Breaking the Spell*, and Frederick Crews's *Follies of the Wise*.

Oxford biologist Richard Dawkins, named Britain's "top intellectual" by a 2005 poll,[71] calls himself, a "militant atheist." Dawkins dismisses God as "an alpha male in the sky"[72] who reveals himself in the Bible to be "the vilest character in fiction."[73] Dawkins's book backs a little away from his two-part television special *The Root of All Evil?* (2006), admitting that religion may not be "the root of all evil" but is very, very bad and mad, full of bigots and zealots. One of Dawkins's favorite quotes is from a physicist-colleague Stephen Weinberg: "for good people to do evil things, it takes religion."[74] Fifty years ago the quote would have read: "for evil people to do good things, it takes religion." Dawkins may define faith as "non-thinking," but he himself fails to think about the three greatest holocausts of the twentieth century (Russia, China, and Germany): two were done by atheists (Russia—Stalin, China—Mao) and one by someone who created a deviant Christian cult (Germany—Hitler).[75]

Close to Dawkins in scientific stature is Daniel C. Dennett. Unlike Dawkins, Dennett wants to talk to Christians. But this is what he wants to say to them: "I am not in awe of your faith. I am appalled by your ignorance, arrogance, by your unreasonable certainty that you have all the answers."[76] Sam Harris's diatribe against religious faith includes the proposition that "some propositions are so dangerous that it may be ethical to kill people for believing them."[77] Frederick Crews mocks Christianity for awkwardly embracing two clashing deities:

one a glutton for praise and a dispenser of wrath, absolution, and grace, the other a curiously inept cobbler of species that need to be periodically revised and that keep getting snuffed out by the very conditions he provided for them. Why, we must wonder, would the shaper of the universe have frittered away some fourteen billion years, turning out quadrillions of useless stars, before getting around to the one thing he really cared about, seeing to it that a minuscule minority of earthling vertebrates are washed clean of sin and guaranteed an eternal place in his company.[78]

*Religious fervor is one of the most destructive forces in today's world.*

ATHEIST JERRY A. COYNE[79]

There is a new joke circulating among unemployed factory workers in the formerly communist countries of Eastern Europe. "Want to know the worst thing about communism?" it is asked. The answer: "postcommunism."

Want to know the worst thing about Christendom?

Post-Christendom. At least, that is what many Christians are saying.

I beg to differ. Christianity is now such a nonfactor in the wider culture that people are becoming open to it as if for the first time.

The best days for Christianity lie in the future, but only if we get rid of Christen*dumb* thinking. In the words of missiologist Alan Hirsch, Constantine "is *still* the emperor of our imaginations."[80] The church must stop chasing the impossible, implausible, and dishonorable dream of re-Christianizing society. It's time for the church to understand that this is a missionary culture and that the church needs to think and act missionally. In China the "gift" of persecution has led the church over the past fifty years to find resources from within that have moved Christianity from two million to eighty million Christians. Who knows what "gifts" God has in store for us in the aftermath of this hurricane?

In fact, there are non-Christians now complaining about the social evils that accompany post-Christendom culture, and hankering after the good old days. We need to hear their voices without heeding their pleas for a return to the past:

> The loss of the religious understanding of the human condition—that man is a fallen creature for whom virtue is necessary but never fully attainable—is a loss, not a gain, in true sophistication. The secular substitute—the belief in the perfection of life on earth by the needless extension of a choice of pleasures—is not merely callow by comparison but much less realistic in its understanding of human nature.[81]

The larger issue of a hurricane of post-Christianity is that many Christian churches are themselves post-Christian, with meager interest in evangelism, with little faith in the Christian tradition itself, but lots of interest in political activism of the liberal persuasion.

## Category 5 STEM[82] Storm: The Global Warming of Post-scale

*Post-scale Means Post-round, Post-cold, Post-human*

***Post-scale:*** It's an old man's hobby to think the world is getting worse: all is decline and decay.

It's a young man's hobby to think the world is better than it has ever been.

The truth is, young and old, the world is getting better, but the dangers the better brings are getting worse. Issues are no longer merely quality of life issues; they are life-or-death issues. The modern doctrine of progress where history moves forward and onward in an upward slope has become as dangerous as it is doubtful.

In a post-progress world, the devil is in the scale more than the devil is in the details. Everything is scalable, but there are thresholds, or tipping points, when scalability suddenly accelerates or becomes more significant. A post-scale world is a very dangerous place. In every one of these problem details, the devil of scale is putting us in a most dangerous place: greenhouse gases, global warming, dying oceans, famine, superbugs, trash, unclean water, air pollution, and epidemics.[83]

No one has made this case for the devil of scale[84] more eloquently than Canadian novelist, essayist, and historian Ronald Wright, who talks about the "progress traps"[85] of technologies that seduce us into the failure that comes from success. "Many of the great ruins that grace the deserts and jungles of the earth are monuments to progress traps, the headstones of civilizations which fell victim to their own success."[86]

To adopt and adapt one of Wright's metaphors, consider yourself a television commercial caveman, a hungry hunter. Before you is a giant woolly mammoth. If all you have to kill that woolly mammoth is a club, a scale-up of a bow and arrow is progress. If all a hungry hunter has to kill a gigantic woolly mammoth is a bow and arrow, a scale-up to a rifle is progress. If all you have to kill a huge woolly mammoth is a rifle, the scale-up of a bazooka is an upscaling of your life. You are now in a fast-food world, with grilled steak instantly possible.

But scale-up one more octave: ratchet up a bazooka to an atomic bomb. You've now met the devil of scale and the progress trap.[87] Use that atomic bomb to kill the giant woolly mammoth, and you've just committed suicide. Or in the words of Wright, "a good bang can be useful; a better bang can end the world."[88] Sometimes to scale-up is not an upscale. There is no small-scale nuclear war.

*Each time history repeats itself, the price goes up.*

GRAFFITI SIGHTED BY RONALD WRIGHT[89]

The price of being human has gone up. Way up. In almost every field of human endeavor, the "bigger bangs" are now post-progress, bringing not merely better quality of life but life-or-death choices. Martin Rees, Astronomer Royal and a world leader in cosmology, has a thousand-dollar bet that "bioerror or bioterror" will kill a million people by 2020.[90] The consequences of the choices we make now are staggering. In fact, these questions are so important that once you start asking them, you almost can't think about anything else.

Let's look at three areas where the scale-up has become post-progress: 1. the GRIN revolution (genetics, robotics, informatics, nano-technology), which has made us post-human; 2. globalization, which has made us post-round; and 3. our care for planet Earth, which has made us post-cold.

***Post-human:*** Dreaming up new moral dilemmas is a favorite perfect storm sport.

> *I believe that for the first time we can begin to map a future which is free of disease and ultimately free of death.*
>
> WILLIAM HASELTINE, CEO OF HUMAN GENOME SCIENCES[91]

In a time of machine-age medicine, we become our machines and our medications. We're all cyborgs now: part born, part made, the born and the made merging into something quite new. Isaac Asimov liked to deny he wrote science fiction. Rather, he wrote "future histories." And those "future histories" have now become present realities. But don't believe me:

> Researchers have engineered mice that are super strong and fast, and live so long that a human equivalent would be at least 200. In Portugal, scientists have implanted cameras connected to electrodes in the brains of blind people. The result? Not only could the subjects see, but they could beam images to each other's minds. In 1998 a neurosurgeon implanted a device into the brain of a "locked-in" patient who couldn't eat, drink, or talk on his own. Before the surgery, the patient could communicate only by blinking his eyes; afterward he could send messages via a computer simply by thinking them out. Over the past decade, the startling advances in nano-science, bioengineering, information technology, and cognitive science—referred to collectively as NBIC have mainstream researchers sounding more and more like singularitarians themselves.[92]

Cyborgs, all.

But don't believe me.

In 2005 the story circulated that Margaret Atwood was becoming a cyborg. It was true. Inspired by her UPS driver's signature machine, Atwood partnered with an inventor and publisher to develop a "signomotron," a remote signing device that would enable her passionate fans (I am one of them)[93] to bring one of her books to any local bookshop, where all you had to do was to press this button and an electronic hand would reproduce her signature that she was scribbling at her home in Canada.[94] Just add a holographic Atwood at the signomotron and you have a picture of our fuzzy future. Matthew Nagel lives in Boston. He was the first human to send an e-mail with his thoughts. He can control a robotic arm with his thoughts. He did this in the summer of 2005.

Cyborgs, all.

Chemical cyborgs, especially. Particularly the young. This is the first generation of medicated children in history. At the first sign of attention deficit, anxiety, obesity or hyperactivity, we intervene pharmaceutically. Richard Louv's book *Last Child in the Woods: Saving Our Children from Nature-Deficit Disorder* (2005), begins with his confession that "the woods were my Ritalin."[95]

Technologies of the past were oriented outward: modify the environment (fire, travel, communication, and so on). Increasingly the technologies of the future are focused inward: modify our minds, metabolisms, and progeny. And the exponential growth of these GRIN technologies[96] can very quickly make us frown.

Our post-human state is a vast cornucopia of blessings and a vast chamber of horrors. Someone has estimated that the twenty-first century as a whole will experience almost one thousand times more technological change than did the twentieth century. Ray Kurzweil says the figure is closer to ten thousand times more change. Kurzweil argues that the twentieth century wasn't one hundred years of progress at today's rate of progress. It was only twenty years. At today's rate of progress, we will see changes equivalent to all the twentieth century in fourteen years, and then seven, and the pace will continue to accelerate because of the explosive nature of exponential growth.

Can Christians keep up with that pace of change? How do we live in a world that's changing faster than individuals and institutions can assimilate the change? Could our multiplying social pathologies and mental health issues be a part of this inability to deal with exponential change?

*Is the speed of technology development exceeding humanity's moral and mental capacities to control it?*

ECONOMIST MAGAZINE[97]

Bill Joy has been called the "Edison of the Internet."[98] One day historians will call Joy's *Wired* essay on "Why the Future Doesn't Really Need Us" the opening salvo of the twenty-first century.[99] According to Joy, scientists are creating a world where, as my Appalachian granddad used to say, "I's scared, and I ain't scared of nothin'."

Joy has carted out from the laboratory into the limelight the curiosities created in the GRIN worlds of genetic engineering,[100] robotics, informatics, and nanotechnology.[101] GRIN technological change is as emblematic as it is problematic: GRIN change is "autocatalytic," that is, self-accelerating and self-replicating. GRIN pathbreaking is truly breathtaking, with far-flung discoveries and far-fetched futures in which, to quote Watts Wacker, "every possibility is uncertain and every uncertainty is a possibility."[102] Our new cathedrals are laboratories, in which science rather than faith gives us answers to the questions of existence.

*This is P2P (peer-to-peer) meets WMD (weapons of mass destruction), producing IDDs (insanely destructive devices).*

LAWRENCE LESSIG[103]

***Post-round:*** Even though I live on an island, I have access unlimited, 24/7, to the entire world. When I sleep, I am umbilically plugged into the whole globe, as messages enter my abode via fax, modem, DSL, cable, satellite dish, e-mail, Tivo, and so on. All problems are now fractal problems, at once local and global.

Or consider the giant-killing power of another postage-stamp plot of planet Earth: Pakistan's northwest frontier and its Afghan hinterland. Whole empires have been brought down by this small pocket of land—the British Empire was badgered for more than one hundred years; the Soviet Union was brought to its knees; the United States received its most terrorizing act from this base. We now live in a world where "remote" has become "remote control."

The phrase *post-round* is inspired by Tom Friedman's postisolationist tract entitled *The World is Flat* (2005),[104] where he argues that advances in technology, travel, and communications have broken down walls between continents, countries, and individuals. Friedman calls globalization "the one big thing" happening in the world that "directly or indirectly influences the politics, environment, geopolitics and economics of virtually every country in the world."[105] In a flat, post-round world, anyone can connect with everyone to the point where it's no more a "you're fired" world (sorry, Donald Trump) but only a "we're wired" world. It's all about connection and collaboration.

Paradoxically, the more global we become, the more tribal differences surge and threaten to blow the global village to smithereens. The smaller our world gets, the more dangerous our world becomes. That's why, the more the world is flat, the more the church needs to be on the edge.

Everything local is now global: SARS, avian flu, terrorism. Because of our interconnectedness and interdependence, the collapse of one system leads to the collapse of all systems. Unlike past disintegrations of civilizations, a disintegration of a particular civilization will cause the disintegration of world civilization. In a post-round world, the peace of Jerusalem or the peace of Jakarta or the peace of Johannesburg is your peace and my peace too. A whole-earth perspective requires a whole-gospel perspective.

*Taken together, the information technologies are eroding the primacy of place, which, ultimately, may be one of the greatest changes the human race has ever experienced.*

VAN WISHARD[106]

Post-round example one: think about how unbelievable it is that a person can write a book in his home country and be condemned and threatened with imprisonment by another country. Before Denmark's cartoonish treatment of Mohammad in February 2006, there was an earlier case that I have heard no one talk about. In 2005, Gerhard Haderer, an Austrian cartoonist was indicted in Greece for blasphemy. His piece of religious satire depicted Christ as a binge-drinking friend of Jimi Hendrix who liked to surf naked while he was high on cannabis.[107]

Haderer did not even know that his forty-page cartoon book, *The Life of Jesus*, had been published in Greece until he received a summons to appear in court in Athens in January (2005). He was charged with blasphemy. Haderer was first given a six-month suspended sentence in absentia, contingent on his appeal. If he lost his appeal, the sentence could be increased to two years.

Haderer's book was the first book to be banned in Greece for more than twenty years. He was the first artist to fall foul of the European arrest warrant system since it was introduced in June 2002.[108]

*Humankind is being brought to a moment where it will have to decide between suicide and adoration.*

TEILHARD DE CHARDIN[109]

Post-round example two: the different memory cultures of three generations have transitioned from a round to a flat Earth. When my grandfather talked about the WWII military service of his two sons (my two uncles), one of whom was part of the Normandy invasion, he talked about something that happened to our country and to his sons.

This is very different than how I talk about my memories of the assassinations of John F. Kennedy, Robert Kennedy, and Martin Luther King, Jr. I can remember exactly where I was when I first heard about these deaths, as well as the eleven murdered Israeli athletes at the 1972 Olympics. And I tell little narratives of where I was when this happened, as if it happened to me.

Why?

Because it did happen to me. Why didn't "the Greatest Generation" craft narratives of their personal experiences of the Normandy invasion or Pearl Harbor?[110] Because it didn't happen to them. They weren't there.[111] In a mediated world, we live in a post-round place "where everything is addressed to us, everything is for us, and nothing is beyond us anymore."[112]

That's why there were all those performance mourners at "the People's Princess" funeral. That's why when a football player scores a touchdown, the fans high five each other, as if they were the ones to score the touchdown.[113] That's why anything that is working in a post-round culture is less a performance ritual than a participation ritual. That's why a post-round world is a karaoke world.

Post-round example three: Have you downloaded Google Earth on your computer? Notice how you can slap it, spin it, turn it upside down or sideways. Every person now has the whole wide world in his or her hands, including the tax assessor checking to see if you have put up any illegal (that is, untaxed) structures on your property.

Or have you visited MySpace or Facebook? Who would have guessed that electronic technology would enhance our ability to eavesdrop on our teenagers' preoccupations?

***Post-cold:*** Global warming is as much a cultural phenomenon as a climactic one of rising sea levels, massive desertification and drought, intensifying storm systems, rapid biological extinction, and so on. For example, the Cold War has devolved into innumerable hot wars, any one of which could destroy planet Earth. And many of these hot wars are fueled by hot spots boiling over in hunger and hopelessness, with more people today stewing in cauldrons of utter poverty than were alive on the entire planet one hundred years ago.[114] As much as poison ivy loves global warming, terrorists flourish in a post-cold world. But what fueled the hatred of the 9/11 bomber Mohamed Atta was less the United States than European disaffection. A German problem, or a French, Dutch, or British problem, can quickly become a global conflagration.[115]

Something serious is happening to our planet. It matters less whether or not humans caused it than what are we going to do about it, we who have been tapped by God to be stewards of planet Earth.

Our beaches are vanishing so fast that beach sand is a new endangered species.

Our rivers are so polluted that you could bottle the water and sell it for poison (Hudson River oysters, anyone?).

Our streams are so full of chemical fertilizer and agricultural runoff that amphibians are growing horns and two heads.

Our seas are so boiling hot that the corals are being bleached dead white.

Our towns are so clogged with cars belching killer gases down concrete-jungle corridors and fattened children lured by jungle gyms to their fast-food deaths that sightings of sky and stars, sun, and moon are becoming ever rarer.

Our animals and plants are going extinct faster than we can name them, twenty-five thousand species a year, in this sixth largest die-off of diversity in human history.

Our rain forests have been so raped and assaulted by our satanic mills grinding away at nature's reproductive systems that humans are liable to sexual harassment lawsuits.

Our jungles are turning into suburban jungle gyms.

Our nature reserves are reversed and ravaged at the first sign of oil, gold, or anything humans deem precious.

Our poorest places on the planet (for example, Bangladesh) face global warming as life threatening, whereas our richest places on the planet face global warming as lifestyle threatening (for example, one average US citizen produces more carbon than ninety-nine Bangladeshis). In a world where a billion people struggle to live on one dollar a day, every cow in the European Union gets $2.50 a day in government subsidy.

The environmental damage caused by the voracious diet of consumerism, whether socialist consumerism in Asia or capitalist consumerism in the Americas, is rearing its ugly head in three arenas: the earth's three natural sinks, its renewable resources, and its nonrenewable resources. The more we squeeze plenitude out of the planet, the more we are choking to death on our plenitude.

*We still have differing cultures and political systems, but at the economic level there is now only one big civilization, feeding on the whole planet's natural capital. We're logging everywhere, fishing everywhere, irrigating everywhere, building everywhere, and no corner of the biosphere escapes our haemorrhage of waste. . . . Every Eldorado has been looted, every Shangri-La equipped with a Holiday Inn.*

RONALD WRIGHT[116]

We are all green now. Even Rick Warren has turned green.[117] You can't be red, white, and blue and not be green. You can't be black or white, brown or yellow, and not be green. You can't be orthodox, East or West, and not be green. Ecumenical Patriarch Bartholomew has officially declared pollution to be a sin.[118]

*1. Three Natural Sinks of Earth, Sea, and Sky*

God provided planet Earth with three cleansing sinks. To demonstrate how we have turned our God-given sinks into contaminated sinkholes, consider the annual spring ritual in Korea of yellow rain. When the toxic, yellow dust blows in, schools close, and people stay indoors or put on their masks.

Yellow rain originates in arid zones like the Taklamakan Desert or the Huangtu Plateau in China. Seasonal winds waft the sand high up into the air, where it is mixed with pollutants and dumped over parts of China, South Korea, and even Japan. As the sand passes over China, it picks up all sorts of poisons—agrochemicals, PCBs, mercury, coal dust, and so on. The winds carry them throughout East Asia, where they are then dumped as yellow rain. The problem is only getting worse, since the environmental degradation of the places where the sand originates is seeing diminished grasslands, eroded soil, and increased desertification. Since China will be opening a new coal-fired power plant every week for the next ten years, there are more and more of these toxins to be picked up with every passing day.

*Today, it is possible to produce a product anywhere, using resources from anywhere, by a company located anywhere to be sold anywhere.*

ECONOMIST MILTON FRIEDMAN[119]

Yellow rain illustrates how our tainting of the two sinkholes of earth and sky can work together to organize something truly awful. But what we have done with our water sink makes an even grimmer story. It's a story of the world's largest public health crisis: clean water.

Twenty-five thousand people die every day in the world from contaminated water and waterborne diseases (principally dysentery): ten thousand to twenty thousand of these twenty-five thousand deaths are children. We have so fouled our water basins that one billion people do not have access to clean drinking water, and the single largest cause of death on this planet is our pollution of drinking water.

Not to mention that 1 in 5 of North Americans drink tap water that has poisonous lead, radiation, herbicides, or even feces in it.

Not to mention the world is running out of fresh water.[120]

If you're thinking future, don't think oil; think water. Water is the oil of the twenty-first century. Since 1950, the world population has doubled, but water use has tripled. We can think of alternative technologies to oil. There are no alternative technologies to water.

The United Nations predicts that by 2050 as many as seven billion people in sixty countries will face water scarcity.[121] A person in an industrialized country uses between 350 and 2000 liters of water daily. A person living in rural Tanzania, for example, may use two to five liters, a truly desperate situation given that people need at least fifty liters of water a day to survive.[122] But this doesn't even begin to address the economics of the situation. Live in Tanzania and you pay 5.7 percent of your daily wages on water. Live in USAmerica and you pay 0.006 percent of your wages on water.[123]

Policy wonks drink their fifty-dollar-per-liter bottled water[124] while figuring out how to reduce the number of people in the world without clean water from 1.2 billion today to five hundred million in 2015. Why isn't the church asking the question why anyone in the world should be drinking polluted water in 2008, much less 2015? Why aren't local churches partnering with local communities around the world to ensure that every child on planet Earth has clean water? Why isn't the church the loudest voice in claiming that water is not a resource but a right, a basic human right that should be available to all people and not a resource subject to the laws of supply and demand?

*2. Renewable Resources: Water, Land, Forests, Fish, and So On*

We are not the first generation in history to lay waste our renewable resources. In fact, some of our earlier food rituals make our tables today appear almost saintly. In the first century, among the Romans, "large red mullet were the most highly sought-after fish in the sea. They were sold live and held in their native element until all the dinner guests had arrived. The poor mullet was then taken out of the water and, before it was handed over to the cook, the company enjoyed the vivid colour changes that take place as fish of this species approach death by asphyxia."[125]

Or consider the Victorian fashion of decorating women's hats not just with feathers, but with whole birds. Birders sometimes did their bird-watching on the streets of New York City, writing down the species of birds they sighted in hats that passed by them. "During two walks along the streets of New York in 1886, the American Museum of Natural History's ornithologist, Frank Chapman, spotted 40 native species of birds including sparrows, warblers, and woodpeckers. But the birds were not flitting through the trees. They had been killed . . . plucked, disassembled or stuffed and painstakingly positioned on three quarters of the 700 women's hats Chapman saw."[126]

But the post-progress nature of a nature exploited, a nature deformed, a nature denatured means that we are fast crossing some point-of-no-return thresholds. The world's fisheries are in deep trouble. The world's rain forests are in deep trouble. If truth be told, the sky is falling, or, put less cock-and-bull, the sun is belching out greenhouse bombs and gases; the sky is shooting deadly darts from guns loaded by the human species. If nature is red in tooth and claw, the claws are mostly ours.

*Pray in a storm, but keep on rowing.*

OLD SAYING

***Cut the carbon:*** Those places and people who have done the least to cause global warming (for example, Bangladesh) will suffer the most from global warming—although any change in the Gulf Stream could have devastating consequences for Europe and North America.[127] Already, 150,000 people die annually from global warming; five million more suffer from health problems.[128] The effect of climate change on health is only recently being understood, with global warnings of dramatic increases in heat-related deaths and disease outbreaks (malaria, dengue fever, cholera) from increased frequencies of tsunamis, hurricanes, and tornadoes. Already Hurricane Katrina has left in its wake a Katrina cough caused by mold, toxins in the air, and oil spills.

In this post-progress world, the weather climate is no longer natural. Our climate is now part of the man-made, human world. That's why the planet needs those man-made humans to cut the carbon with Manhattan Project urgency.

*3. Nonrenewable Resources: Oil, Minerals, and So On*

Our fossil fuel dependency is so severe, and we love oil so much, that we even eat oil (we use it to fertilize our food).

Something is wrong with the American dream. For too many people the American dream has become a nightmare, a suicide machine. Wendell Berry calls it the "wheel of death."[129] The more we want, the more unsatisfied we feel, which makes us want more, which makes us feel even more incomplete. We've created more than a sorry mess. We're threatened by a ghastly nightmare of our own making.

Bruce Springsteen popularized the term in his song "Born to Run." Brian McLaren's book *Everything Must Change* (2007) was originally titled *Jesus and the Suicide Machine*. Others using this metaphor of suicide include Ronald Wright and Edward Echlin of East Sussex, England, the former who talks about the status quo as a "suicide machine,"[130] the latter who talks about our role as humans in the "assisted suicide of Earth."[131] *Suicide* is more than a metaphor when the suicide rate among women increased 200 percent in the past two decades, when teen suicides jumped 300 percent between 1960 and 1990.

Our current way of life is both metaphorically and literally suicide. It is more than crazy; it is suicide.

When our modern scientific strategies are, by definition, predatory—it is more than crazy; it is suicide. Here is Audubon in his essay "My Style of Drawing Birds" describing how he drew a kingfisher:

> I pierced the body of the Fishing bird and fixed it on the board,—another Wire passed above his upper Mandible was made to hold the head in a pretty fair attitude. Smaller Skewers fixed the feet according to my notions, and even common pins came to my assistance in the placing of the legs and feet—The last Wire proved a delightful elevator to the Bird's Tail, and at Last there Stood before me the real . . . Kings Fisher.[132]

The real kingfisher, huh? Emily Dickinson warned about dissecting a lark to find how a lark makes its music in these words: "Split the

Lark—and you'll find the Music—," she says. "Bulb after Bulb, in Silver rolled—," but in so doing you have killed the singer and the song: "Scarlet Experiment! Sceptic Thomas! / Now, do you doubt that your Bird was true?"[133]

When we organize around honoring technology as our major God, it is more than crazy; it is suicide.

When we organize around business making money as the ultimate good, it is more than crazy; it is suicide.

When Mother Nature is fated to lose her maternal reference because of the wrath we are unleashing in her from our abuse, neglect, and matricide, it is more than crazy; it is suicide.

When bad health is good business, it is more than crazy; it is suicide.[134]

When insurance companies will pay for dialysis, but not for consultations with nutritionists, who can help diabetics not need the dialysis, it is more than crazy; it is suicide.

When human actions may be well-intentioned but are undertaken with no real understanding of their consequences, it is more than crazy; it is suicide.

When we are no longer organizing human culture around the values that will allow the human spirit to survive, it is more than crazy: it is suicide.

When people are feeling that we have already made such a mess of planet Earth that we might as well make the most of what we still have and enjoy it while we can, it is more than crazy; it is suicide.

Only truth can turn off the suicide machine. We must cure the status quo with truth. We must be about the mission of jamming the suicide machine with truth.

# CHAPTER TWO

# Man Overboard!

GREG GLATZ *(Canada)*

Jesus remained calm in the center of the storm, so calm that he lay *asleep* in the stern as the waves washed over the boat.[1] Unlike their master, the disciples feared the storm, and fear has bedeviled the church ever since. The church is afraid of storms. It prefers the tranquility of calm seas. It seeks the protection of safe harbors when storms arise.

And yet, the church needs to *sail out*, not sell out or wimp out. Humanity is drowning, and its cries will go unheard unless the church braves the stormy waters. Today, the church is being sent out by Jesus, propelled by the power of the Holy Gust, to rescue lost souls drowning in an aquatic culture of postmodernity, post-Christendom, and post-scale. This perfect storm presents incredible challenges to the church, but these challenges can strengthen and refine the church, rather than shipwreck her. For this reason, the greatest days of the church may lie ahead.

How do ships make it through the storms? Conventional wisdom dictates a defensive approach: batten down the hatches, shut the windows and portholes, stow the gear, and pump the bilge dry. Then, point the ship into the waves, tie the anchor, tether the crew, and hold on for dear life.[2] Unfortunately, these measures are inadequate in severe storms, as the Fastnet and Sydney-Hobart race disasters of the late twentieth century made tragically clear.

The Fastnet Race, one of the United Kingdom's premier yachting tournaments, spans 608 nautical miles, beginning off Cowes, traveling to Fastnet Rock off the southwest coast of Ireland, and then back to Plymouth via the south side of the Isles of Scilly. In 1979, violent storm winds descended on the race, imperiling over three hundred yachts. By the time the storm subsided, twenty-four crews had abandoned ship, five yachts had sunk, and fifteen people had died. Only eighty-five boats completed the race.[3]

The Sydney Hobart Yacht Race, another prestigious sailing event, was also marred by disaster. Hosted by the Cruising Yacht Club of Australia, the race begins in Sydney on Boxing Day and finishes in Hobart, Tasmania, some 630 nautical miles south. Ominously referred to as "Hell on High Water," the race lived up to its name in 1998, when hell unleashed its fury in full. Competitors ran headlong into a severe, deadly storm. Winds of hurricane strength whipped the waves to heights of thirty feet and more. Five boats were lost at sea and six people lost their lives. Of the 115 boats that began the race, only forty-four made it to Hobart.[4]

Conventional storm maneuvers failed to protect the ships and crew lost in the Fastnet and Hobart race disasters. Donald Jordan, a mechanical engineer and sailing enthusiast, analyzed data from the Fastnet and Hobart races along with the results of testing conducted by the U.S. Coast Guard. He began a quest for a new storm sailing strategy by focusing his attention on the position of the ship relative to the wave. Typically, skippers point their ships *into* the waves to reduce speed. This protects the ship against its number one threat: breaking waves. These waves set upon a ship with extreme speed and height, lift the boat to the crest of a wave, accelerate it to full wave speed, and hurl it onto the waters below, where it is smashed to splinters. Pointing a ship into the waves reverses the positions of the streamlined bow and wedge-shaped stern. This tactic forces the waves to work against the hull's hydrodynamic design, effectively reducing the ship's speed.

However, this tactic also reduces the ship's maneuverability. When a ship sails backwards, it works against its rudder and hull design, which makes it susceptible to yawing—turning broadside to the waves. When a ship yaws, it becomes liable to capsize, at which point the chances of righting itself are virtually nil.

Jordan's research led to the creation of a series drogue, a submersible dragging device with an innovative twist.[5] The twist is an exquisitely simple but especially effective design. The series drogue consists of a hundred or more small fabric cones—mini parachutes—attached along the length of a double-braided nylon rope. The rope is weighted on the tail end by a length of chain that anchors the drogue under water. The other end of the rope is deployed from the stern (rear) of the ship.

The drogue itself is not new. Sailors have attached dragging devices to their ships for centuries. However, the serial design of Jordan's drogue (many cones along the length of a rope) was revolutionary. The series of cones provided exceptional drag over the directional length of the rope. This removed the necessity of pointing the ship into the waves and allowed the skipper to work with, rather than against, the design of the hull and rudder.

Even in severe storm conditions, a series drogue can slow a ship to one or one and a half knots—a speed so low that the crew is not required to steer the boat![6] As such, the series drogue is a very effective solution to breaking waves. If a ship is approached from behind by a large breaking wave, the wave briefly accelerates the boat until the drag of the series drogue kicks in, decelerates the boat, and allows the breaking wave to pass harmlessly underneath the hull. Jordan aptly notes that the series drogue is truly "the sailor's airbag."

Jordan's series drogue has been used at sea for over twenty years. Used in countless storms, including numerous hurricanes, no boat has ever been damaged and no crew injured when a series drogue has been deployed. Because the drag of the drogue allows the crest of each wave to pass quickly under the ship, the ship spends more time in the trough between the waves, where the wind is weaker and the water less volatile. In contrast to the conventional nerve-wracking practice of steering a ship backwards against the waves, skippers can relax when a series drogue is deployed. The crew is unneeded and "sleeps through the remainder of the storm in relative comfort."[7] Ironically, however, the series drogue has not been widely adopted. The reason? People don't want to spend one thousand dollars for a series drogue when a conventional drogue costs much less.

Counting the cost is near and dear to the heart of Jesus.[8] The church needs to count the cost of discipleship. It needs to ask, "What does it cost to follow Jesus into the perfect storm?" What will the church need to give up—and what will it need to gain—to prepare itself for the ultimate rescue mission?

The answer to these crucial questions lies in the oppositional relationship between fear and love. You cannot fear and love. You must give up one to take up the other. As John so vividly states, "There is no fear in love, but perfect love casts out fear; for fear has to do with punishment, and whoever fears has not reached perfection in love."[9] *Love—agape* in the New Testament writings[10]—is the way to perfection. It is the new commandment, the greatest commandment, and the royal law. And so, when the church chooses rightly the way of love, it must also choose to surrender fear in all its forms and manifestations. This is, at the most fundamental level, what it means to count the cost.

In the Gospels and Epistles, *agape* is a robust love, a brave and bold love. It often represents a love that is willing to make the ultimate sacrifice:

> For God so loved the world that he gave his only Son, so that everyone who believes in him may not perish but may have eternal life.[11]

> Christ loved us and gave himself up for us[12]

The ultimate sacrifice is required also from the church. Those who name the name of Christ are "crucified with Christ."[13] It is a crucifixion of "the flesh with its passions and desires."[14] At issue here is not passion and desire per se, but fleshly, self-serving passions and desires that stand in opposition to love. Fuelled by fear, these passions and desires give rise to enmities, strife, jealousy, anger, quarrels, dissensions, factions, envy, and so on.[15] It is these destructive forces within, not the maelstrom without, that will sink our ship.

And so, "I die daily"[16] becomes the rallying cry of every Christian mariner. With every act of self-denial we deploy a drogue, cone by cone—crucifixion by crucifixion—beneath the stormy seas. Each time we crucify the flesh with its passions and desires we throw our "old man"[17] overboard and allow the weight of our crucified selves to work for the safety of the ship. Our drogue is weighted by the anchor of Christ's own crucifixion. As the drogue's metal chain enters the water first and keeps the drogue submerged, so the crucifixion of Christ, who is "the first fruits of those who have died,"[18] weights our crucifixions in the waters of the perfect storm. We follow Jesus, who bore the cross before us.[19] As such, dying to ourselves is never a self-aggrandizing, autonomous act; it is the process of being conformed to the image of Christ.[20]

As the fair wind carries the church into the foul winds of the perfect storm, it will be more important than ever to throw the old man overboard. Paradoxically, when we die to ourselves we live to love another day. The drogue of self-sacrificial love steadies us through the wind and waves of post-modernism, post-Christendom, and post-scale. We remain calm and at peace as the storm rages round us. For now, our lives are hidden in Christ: we will find them again when Christ is revealed.[21] Someday, on the last day when the perfect storm subsides, God will transform the "body of our humiliation" and conform it to the body of Christ's glory.[22] Then we will be complete, *telios*—perfect. Until then, we complete what is lacking in Christ's afflictions.[23]

> He prayeth best, who loveth best
> All things both great and small;
> For the dear God who loveth us,
> He made and loveth all.[24]

CHAPTER THREE

# In Sync with Jesus and the First Perfect Stormers

STEPHAN JOUBERT *(South Africa)*

*She always walked against the stream. When everyone fled the city, she was the only one who walked in the opposite direction.*

A BISHOP AT MOTHER THERESA'S FUNERAL

## Chaos in Heaven!

One day unexpected chaos broke out in heaven—holy chaos! News had broken that Jesus would be going to earth. At first, moments of stunned silence deafened the praise and worship of heaven. Then, everybody started talking at the same time. Amidst this holy chaos, the archangel Michael, spoke out: "My Lord, why? The earth is definitely not worthy of your personal presence. Let me go in your place. With my sword I will subdue the nations in a divine instant."

Jesus refused his offer, as well as an equally tempting offer by all the other angels for a swift heavenly *coup d'etat* on earth. He would personally undertake the dangerous journey into the terrible storm that raged on earth.

The angels in charge of heaven's wardrobe said, "Dear Lord, at least allow us to pack your suitcase for the journey. We'll prepare a golden halo and fine kingly robes for you." Jesus turned this offer down once again. Heavenly robes were definitely not suited for his trip to earth! Actually, nothing heaven had to offer for this perilous journey appealed to Jesus, especially not the golden crown, the throne, or the red carpets.

Some angels dared to ask, "Have you chosen clothes similar to those of the high priest in Jerusalem?" But another cup of heavenly cold water hit them right between the eyes. Priestly garments wouldn't work for Jesus either. The only clothes suitable for his journey were those of the lowest of the low on earth. Slaves would inspire his earthly attire.

The garments of a slave for the Child of the King of the universe? Yes! This is the ultimate paradox, the divine mystery, and the unopened secret of Christianity. The heart of heaven's Servant-King couldn't refuse the opportunity of an eternity to serve those on earth.

## The God-need Storm

Why did Jesus come to earth? Why didn't Jesus remain in heaven? Why did he want so desperately to be among us?

Jesus came to earth because a storm was raging throughout the world—a storm known as *God-need*. God-need is

- To stand alone in the wind and tempestuous weather.
- To feel alienated and alone, even when surrounded by throngs of people.
- To be hungry and thirsty, even though you indulge your physical appetites every day.
- To be cut off from your heavenly umbilical cord. It means missing the route home because you missed out on Jesus.
- To be a lifelong prisoner within the safe harbor of religious environments. God-need is to live in spiritual arrogance because you believe you have all the answers locked up in your well-preserved belief systems.

***Breaking news:*** *God-need* is also a neurological fact inherent to *Homo sapiens*. In the early 1990s, neuroscientists determined that the temporal lobes of our brain have a so-called *God-spot,*[1] located just behind our temples. Our God-spot is activated when we engage in spiritual activities. Thus, we are biologically wired to long for God. Our brains are designed with a *God-need* that constantly craves for his touch! We have an inbuilt God-thirst deep within us. It is a lifelong need that never dissipates.[2]

Religious professionals could not quell this God-need storm. They could not rescue the victims. In fact, they often intensified the devastating effects of the storm. Only Jesus, and those who follow him into the storm, can offer salvation to people drowning in a sea of God-need. Jesus didn't re-invent the old. He didn't rehash the status quo. He established a new covenant and with it a new status of honor, a new map of reality, and a new next of kin.

## A New Status of Honor: The Slave

*The only difference between a slave and a dog is that a slave has the ability to speak.*

ARISTOTLE[3]

*Slaves are agricultural implements with human voices.*

VARRO[4]

In the first-century world where Jesus' feet touched the ground, *honor* was the pivotal value. Isocrates, the Athenian orator around the time of Aristotle (*Ad Dem.* 43), placed honor above personal safety. Quintillian (*Institutes* 3.8.1), the well-known rhetorician of the first century, stated that the "honorable" was the fundamental key in persuading people to follow certain courses of action, or to avoid them. Honor was valued more highly than truth; it was a far more valuable commodity than wealth. The lack of honor turned individuals and groups into objects of scorn, insult, disgrace and, eventually, into total outcasts.

Honor could be ascribed or acquired. Ascribed honor derived from one's birth into a family of good social standing or was bestowed by people of higher standing on their inferiors. Acquired honor resulted from public interactions, called "challenge and riposte." People of equal social standing constantly challenged each other according to clearly defined rules to gain more honor in the eyes of the public. No wonder that ancient Mediterranean society was regarded as an *agonistic* culture, because all social interactions outside one's family or circle of friends were seen as contests for honor.[5]

Despite the world's preoccupation with honor, Jesus assumed the status of a slave. He clothed himself in rags instead of riches. He divested himself of honor and identified himself with the dishonorable. Approximately one of every four people in the Roman Empire was a slave. Slaves were the floor rags of the ancient world. Prisoners of war and others who could not settle their debts were sold off as slaves to the wealthy and the powerful. Others were born into slavery. Slaves faced a harsh, often brutal, existence. The rich regarded slaves as expendable assets, their market value determined by their appearance, learning, physical power, and skills. Slaves had no rights. Plutarch (A.D. 100) mentions that some slaves were not permitted to speak unless they were addressed directly. According to Aristotle (*Pol.* 1.2.14), even the bodies of freemen and slaves were different—"the latter strong for necessary service, the former erect and unserviceable for such occupation, but serviceable for a life of citizenship."[6]

In the hymn of Philippians 2:5-11, Paul sings of Jesus' earthbound rescue mission: his traveling clothes, his stopovers, his final destination, and the eternal impact of his trip to earth. Paul describes the Savior, first and foremost, as a slave:

> Let the same mind be in you that was in Christ Jesus,
> who, though he was in the form of God,
>     did not regard equality with God
>     as something to be exploited,
> but emptied himself,
>     taking the form of a slave,
>     being born in human likeness.
> And being found in human form,
>     he humbled himself

and became obedient to the point of death—
even death on a cross.

Therefore God also highly exalted him
and gave him the name
that is above every name,
so that at the name of Jesus
every knee should bend,
in heaven and on earth and under the earth,
and every tongue should confess
that Jesus Christ is Lord,
to the glory of God the Father.

Here we have the "mind" of Christ turned into action. His *fronesis*, his deepest convictions, turned him into a full-fledged slave. This crucial choice took him all the way to the cross to die a horrible death. However, at this point the story of Jesus, like a hyperbole turned upside down, he made a gigantic reversal as God exalted him and gave him a name above all names. So powerful is this name that all will eventually bow down and confess that he is Lord.

Jesus' life and death created a new storm strategy for his followers—a highly dangerous but adventurous new way to walk on stormy seas! When Jesus entered our stormy world, he sacrificed his divine honor. He became a slave in order to save the slaves. He associated with the lowest of the low. He emptied himself. And, as a slave, he carried the sins of the world on his shoulders. Those who follow Jesus into the storm—his fellow storm chasers—must be willing to do the same.

## A New Map of Reality: The Kingdom of God

Religious power in Palestine during the first century was embedded in the priests of Jerusalem, a powerful minority of elites who controlled all facets of Jewish life.[7] They consciously split reality into two spheres and categorized all persons, animals, food, time, and space in terms of this distinction between holy and unholy. Holy people included, in hierarchical order, priests, Levites, full-blooded Israelites, illegitimate children of priests, proselytes (non-Jewish converts), and so on. The impure in Israel included all those born of adulterous unions, children of prostitutes, eunuchs, and others with deformed sexual features. Non-Jewish people were considered an abomination. They did not even register on Israel's purity scales. Contact with them was to be avoided at all costs.

According to the Mishnah document, *Mo'ed*, time was also classified from the holy to the ordinary according to the following hierarchy: Shabbat (Sabbath was the holiest day on Israel's calendar), Pesachim (Feast of Passover), Yoma (Day of Antonement), Sukkot (Feast of Tabernacles), Yom Tov (Festival Days), Rosh ha-Shana (Feast of the New Year), Taanit (Days of Fasting), Megillah (Feast of Purim), and Mo'ed Katan (Mid-festival Days).

Space was also classified according to various degrees of holiness. The holiest place on earth was the temple in Jerusalem with the Holy of Holies, which marked the center of the temple, which marked the center of Jerusalem, which marked the center of Palestine, which marked the center of the world.

When Jesus started his ministry in Galilee, it became clear that he did not share the same map of reality as the religious experts of his day. He was considered a transgressor of the Sabbath, the most important day on the sacred calendar. Jesus ignored the boundaries separating holy and impure people by touching lepers[8] and corpses.[9] He did nothing to prevent hemorrhaging women[10] and prostitutes[11]—also unclean people—from touching him. In fact, he never considered himself defiled by contact with unclean people. It actually worked the other way round: his touch made them clean! Jesus transgressed Jewish *kashrut* regulations or dietary laws by not expecting of his disciples to keep the washing rites before meals.[12] He ate with despised persons such as tax collectors and sinners.[13] He interacted with non-Jews who didn't make it into Israel's circles of holiness.[14]

Equally challenging was Jesus' reconfiguration of Jewish sacred space. Although he acknowledged the role of the temple in Jerusalem,[15] he made it clear that this static holy site, set aside as God's special dwelling place, was now redundant.[16] He inaugurated a new era of worshiping God anywhere in spirit and truth. Jesus himself became the new sacred space that replaced Jerusalem's temple and all its bloody sacrifices[17]—shocking words for those who believed the sacrificial system in Jerusalem formed the cornerstone of Israel's faith!

Jesus did not accept the religious elite's map of reality because it did not demand a change of heart (repentance). Their map reinforced nationalistic and patriarchal ideologies at the expense of non-Israelites, women, outcasts, the impure, children, and so on. Their map of reality left many out in the deep to drown and created religious safe harbors for the privileged few. Jesus proclaimed a new map of reality—the kingdom of God. In the kingdom of God, the unwelcome were welcomed; the first became last and the last became first; the greatest became the least and the least became greatest. No wonder the religious establishment killed Jesus. His new map of reality left them empty-handed.

## A New Next of Kin: The Household of God

The family formed the backbone of the ancient Mediterranean world. All work, religion, culture, and politics testified to the centrality of kinship and family life. The first-century world was clearly a dyadic, or collectivistic, culture: identities were inherently associated with the clan or family. *So and so* was always the son of or the father of or the daughter or brother or acquaintance of . . . . People were valued not because of their uniqueness, as is typical in Western culture today, but in terms of their dyadic relations with larger, honorable family groups.

Jesus founded a new household of God. This household was not constituted along biological lines: to become a brother or a sister or a mother of Jesus, people had to do the will of the heavenly Father. Loyalty to the household of God often led to conflict between biological fathers and sons, and so on. The new family of Jesus had only one agenda: to become perfect stormers with Jesus, searching for the lost and welcoming would-be family members. People who became part of this new household were accepted on the basis of who they were (followers of Jesus, brothers and sisters), not on the basis of the rank or status acquired through patronage or politics.[18] The new household of God was mobile and dynamic. Wherever Jesus walked, talked, or ate, strangers found refuge in his presence. As this new household took shape around him, nobodies, has-beens, and those very low on the honor scale, such as women, sinners, and children, were welcomed.[19] They were allowed to participate equally in God's overflowing goodness.

One of the most beautiful examples of the household of God comes from Thessalonica, a city in the Roman province of Macedonia. According to Acts 17, Paul probably spent less time in Thessalonica than any other city he visited. In spite of this, the church in Thessalonica was one of Paul's most successful church-plants. I've searched for the keys to Paul's church-planting strategies in 1 Thessalonians, but I've found no lengthy discussions of leadership structures, the nature of their worship gatherings, or their liturgies, and so on. Instead, it's all about faith, hope, and love! Paul tells us so in 1 Thessalonians 1:3: "remembering before our God and Father your work of *faith* and labor of *love* and steadfastness of *hope* in our Lord" (emphasis added). In the apostle's best-seller letter to the Corinthians, he writes at length about this triad of nonnegotiable Christian values.[20] But here in his earliest letter we see that, from the beginning, Paul hammered these simple, life-changing principles deep into the hearts of his young churches. Immediately, they started imitating Paul and the Lord as their role models.[21] Within a short space of time, people in various Roman provinces were hearing about this young and vibrant Christian community.[22] In fact, they were accused of turning the world upside down.[23] What an awesome crime to commit!

## The Storm Chasing Goes On

Jesus' crucifixion was supposed to bring an abrupt end to storm chasing. However, as soon as Jesus was safely back in heaven, crowned again with heavenly glory and a new name, his earthly followers received the storm-chasing Spirit. They took on the status of slaves. They preached the kingdom of God. And they remained the new household of God, just as Jesus had envisioned. They did not meet in formal places of worship, nor did they put up sanctuaries throughout the Roman Empire. Holy buildings, formal ritualized meetings, official priests, theologians—these things never signified the first followers of Jesus. They were a new kind of family! They thrived on healthy relationships, frequent, unstructured contact, and constant caring for each other.

Jerusalem was the first harbor of a large gathering of storm chasers (Acts 1–7). This community is held up today as an example for all modern churches to imitate, but I don't believe we're meant to imitate their behavior slavishly. We're meant to align ourselves with their storm-chasing values. The Jerusalem church, as well as the second biggest church in early Christianity, Antioch, were exceptions to the rule in terms of the actual size of most early Christian communities. Early Christian groups were never larger than about sixty to one hundred members. The architecture and size of ordinary Roman houses did not allow for large gatherings of hundreds of people at a time. More importantly, due to their identity as new households of God, the first Christians did not anticipate or envision meetings of such large groups. Families lose their cohesion when they grow too big. One-on-one relationships flourish in smaller, face-to-face situations. That's why the early church did not opt for the formalized meetings of the synagogue or the structured meetings of the Roman guilds, funeral clubs, and other voluntary associations. From their daily doorsteps, the first followers of Jesus affected their surroundings as full-time market place missionaries.

## Ban All Religious Aquariums

Too many churchgoers hide out in religious aquariums (churches!), where everything is neatly under control:

- The *spiritual temperature* (highly predictable gatherings in religious comfort zones),
- The *feeding times* (designated, convenient times on Sundays),
- The *maintenance personnel* (friendly, paid church officials),
- The *right filters* to keep the water clean (safe church programs and activities that make no one feel uncomfortable).

Do you know what happens to fish that spend long periods in aquariums and are released into the sea? They die! The same happens to glass-sheltered, churchgoing people who suddenly find themselves among nonchurchgoers. They compromise on their principles. Some even abandon their faith.

Too many monuments without momentum
Cerebral cathedrals
Frozen religious professionals
In-church fighting
Worship wars

This while the world is becoming flatter

God-need is growing bigger
And believers ever thinner
The storm's intensity is worsening
It seems as if the "church" has been washed away

Thank God!

Follow Jesus! Just do it! Become a storm chaser. Stop wasting precious time in religious safe harbors. Stop planning irrelevant religious activities to save a few somebodies, someday, in Saint Elsewhere. Turn the world upside down. Set new standards. Talk a new talk. Walk a different walk. Become a living expression of Jesus. He is always at his best in the midst of the storm. Stay close to Jesus, even as he heads deeper into the storm.

## CHAPTER FOUR

# Seasoned Sailors

ALAN JAMIESON (*New Zealand*)

*They that go down to the sea in ships,*
*that do business in great waters;*
*these see the works of the LORD,*
*and his wonders in the deep.*

PSALM 107:23-24 KJV

Out my study's window, the hillside, littered with old wooden homes, spreads down toward a thin isthmus of land that separates the harbor bays from the southern coast. Beyond, there is only the southern ocean, nothing but the sea between the South Pole and us. Cold weather regularly comes from this direction bashing the hillside, driving rain and wind on our windows with polar ferocity. The worst of these storms stole our garage. Blown apart. Now, nearly forty years on, only the concrete foundations remain.

It was April 10, 1968, when the worst recorded storm in New Zealand's history hit the capital city of Wellington. The inter-island ferry, *Wahine*,[1] was nearing the harbor on her regular sailing from Christchurch, the largest city in the South Island, to the southernmost city of the North Island. It had been a normal sailing. Although some passengers were feeling the effects of seasickness, the overnight ferry had traveled up the east coast of the South Island without incident. There was no reason for any of the experienced crew to show particular concern.[2]

Just before 6 A.M., as the ship was approaching the narrow harbor entrance, Captain Robertson arrived back on the bridge. Visibility was good, despite the slowly increasing rain. The weather report for the harbor was fifty-knot winds, gusting to sixty knots. The wind and white-capped waves would not have any appreciable effect on the *Wahine*'s movement as the powerful turboelectric engines of the three-year-old ship thrust her through the Cook Strait. The lights that guided ships into the harbor were clearly visible.[3]

When visibility began decreasing, the bridge crew noticed the radar suddenly ceased to function. Captain Robertson ordered a reduction in speed. Suddenly, the ship started to sheer to port heading rapidly toward the reef. The captain ordered a change of direction. The ship didn't respond. He ordered full ahead on both engines to increase speed and bring back the steering. Still the *Wahine* swung. By now the ship was in the narrowest part of the rock-fringed harbor and visibility was getting worse. The *Wahine*, its 123 crew, 610 passengers, and two stowaways, were suddenly in serious trouble.

On land, a few kilometers away, winds of 130 to 140 miles-an-hour were being recorded as a hurricane's full force hit the city.[4] The *Wahine* crew fought thirty- to forty-foot waves in zero visibility without radar. Captain Robertson had nothing to navigate with but his instinct and feeling. At times he sensed the ship was approaching rocks ahead and ordered her astern. Other times, he felt she was near the Pencarrow Coast astern and ordered her ahead. Some twenty-five minutes after the vessel started sheering uncontrollably to port, those on the bridge were still without a clue on the ship's exact position in the channel. In the circumstances, it seemed incredible that she had evaded the rocks for so long.[5]

At 6:33 A.M. the captain ordered full astern on starboard. It was instinct, pure and simple, which decided him on this course. As he later told the court of inquiry: "You sometimes get the feeling in a fog that you are getting close to the beach. You stop and go astern and when you check up later you find you have missed the beach by a few feet. These things happen."[6] Then another rogue wave hit, and the ship was thrown on to the rocks. It was precisely 6:41 A.M.[7] Suddenly, every seasoned sailing skill, every ounce of experience, and all the courage they could muster was required of the captain and crew.

## The Need for Seasoned Sailors

Anyone can be a fair-weather sailor. When the harbor is calm and the breeze gentle, it is dead easy to play captain. But when the storm hits, it demands more than fair-weather experience. It calls for seasoned sailors. The storms approaching the church demand seasoned sailors of faith with as much experience, skill, intuition, courage, fast thinking, and thoroughness as Captain Robertson and the crew of the *Wahine*.

Seasoning is an interesting image. It comes with a double meaning. First, seasoning suggests "coming into efficient or sound condition by exposure, use and lapse of time."[8] In this sense, seasoned sailors of faith are those who have weathered the storms and seasons of Christian faith and life's realities. Second, seasoning is the way we enhance or improve the flavor of food, by adding or by rubbing in salt, for example. In this sense, seasoned sailors are those who have been improved by life struggles and faith crises—people who have had the salt rubbed in many times before.

I learned to row in a dinghy tied to the end of the jetty. Backwards and forwards, I rowed to the extent of my tether in either direction. When I became somewhat accomplished at rowing, steering, and balance, I was allowed off the safety line, but only in the bay and only while the weather was calm. Without the tether, I could explore further afield. I could practice rowing in a straight line while facing in the opposite direction to the one I was traveling. I could practice steering the boat into the beach, along the rocky edges, and up to the steps of the jetty. Having mastered these skills, a slightly bigger boat and a small motor provided more opportunities for experience. Now trips beyond the bay, deeper water, rougher waves and longer periods on the water could be ventured. With each step I was slowly learning to sail a boat myself.

My boating experience stopped there. I never learned to sail or to be competent in anything but a small dinghy with a small outboard motor. Occasionally, I've gone boating in friends' boats and had a bash at steering. But there has always been someone more experienced alongside if things get rough.

I would suggest that too many of us are about as experienced and skillful in the living of our faith as I am in sailing a boat. We've started out. We've played in the shallows, and we have learned some basics. We know a little bit about Christian faith. We've prayed a little, understood a little theology, read a little, and been involved in practical, hands-on mission work a little. But we are no more seasoned sailors of the oceans of Christian faith than I am a seasoned boatie.

And sadly, the leadership and structures of most churches have not encouraged us, or even expected us, to go further. Even more sadly, most churches are led by people who are no more seasoned sailors of the oceans of faith than we are ourselves. Eugene Peterson has repeatedly pointed out today's pastors and church leaders seem to have more in common with managers and executives from the business world than spiritual leaders to whom people can turn with confidence in the worst of life's experiences.[9] Managerial and executive experience, even our efforts to strengthen our Christian faith, seem woefully inadequate for the storms that are coming.

The church in Western contexts has been lulled by the calm between storms. As modernity's winds of rationalism have faded, we have entered a false complacency. It has been too easy to abandon the deeper demands of Christian living. It has been too easy to abandon the hard work of the study.[10] It has been too easy to abandon the rigors of dedicated long-term involvement in community mission. But mostly we have abandoned the soul-searching life of prayer that draws us beyond the shallows and immerses us in the storms of pain, injustice, our personal poverty, and the rawest emotions and experiences of life.

Returning to the metaphor of sailing, too many of us have simply abandoned ship and begun to live as functional atheists who happen to attend church from time to time. Others have stuck with the ship (living a Christian ethic and life) but left the demands of discernment and decision-making to others on the bridge. As the perfect storm approaches, I fear we, in the Western church, are woefully ill prepared.

Seasoned sailors will be needed, not deserters and passengers. Sadly, few seasoned sailors seem to be in view.

## Becoming Seasoned Sailors

For the last ten years, I have been researching how people grow in Christian faith; research that began out of asking why people leave Christian churches. This research has involved tracking people over a period of five years as they navigated their journeys of faith beyond the institutional forms of church. Such leavers are a growing sector of the Christian community. Many of these people leave because they sense an inner compulsion to move beyond the safe harbors[11] that churches provide and encourage. They sense a strong urge to venture into the deeper waters of faith and life.

They sense a call to head out beyond the safe markers of many churches into the open seas.[12] They describe these journeys as similar to Jesus' journeys into the wildernesses and the darkest places of faith—the places where faith becomes deeply interior. These are places where the outer comforts, supports, and trappings are stripped away and all that is left, all that survives, is a personal encounter with a loving and accepting God.

It is in the personal storms, the real crucibles of personal faith, that seasoned sailors are shaped. Such seasoning cannot be rushed.[13] As the Spirit of God calls us to explore beyond safe waters, we are thrust into deep periods of doubt; periods of reassessing what we believe; periods of deconstructing our faith and stripping us back to the bare essentials; periods of pain, suffering, and grief; periods dominated by failure, our own and others. Yet in these storms we can come to see through the darkness a profound, albeit sketchy, image of God at work in our lives. Traversing such storms are dark days, as Mike Riddell states

> The dark days are just beginning. Before you emerge into the light again you will be stripped to the core. You will rage and scream at God. You will retreat into a cocoon of sorrow and breathe in slow motion. The color will drain from the sky, the meaning from life. As a plough tears through hard earth, your heart will be broken up. You will make friends with pain, nursing it as the child of grief. Utter emptiness fills the earth, and the valley appears to contain nothing but the echo of your own cry.

———

> Surely God has left you. The road which seemed to be heading somewhere has become a dead end. A mocking maze with no exit.[14]

There is no substitute for the storms that dislodge our externally focused faith, propelling us toward a deeper, quieter, self-owned, and personally experienced sense of Christ within. For some, the period of riding the storms is relatively short-lived until calm-weather faith emerges again. For others, the storm clouds become an ongoing reality. They simply ride from one storm to another. The God they look to is Christ found in the midst of the storm.

## Seasoned through Being Becalmed

Ironically, although our interiority of faith is gained through the storms, it is also gained in those times of being becalmed. When we are becalmed, the illusions of progress are demolished. The old ways of prayer, worship, and Bible reading become dry and stale. The church services and preaching that used to encourage us, teach us, and inspire us become barren ground. God seems to extinguish one means of feeding our faith in order to make us hungry, even starving, for new ways.

Saint John of the Cross knew what it was to be becalmed with no hint of God around. He taught that at first we sense that God is completely absent—that God has deserted us. But slowly we come to realize that God is not absent. God is there, but we couldn't recognize God or see God at work because we didn't know where to look or listen. We cannot sense God because we are used to God coming in a particular way. Now that way is void and empty, but God nevertheless comes to us in new ways—if we can only perceive them. When we are becalmed, we learn to wait.

As we wait, we begin to understand that we are part of something much bigger than we had realized. We understand that our part is very small and very insignificant, yet crucially important. This slow dawning brings a mixture of awe, shame, and excitement. In this way, our love for God and others is deepened as "God painfully parts the fibres of our being to penetrate the very marrow of our souls."[15]

## Seasoned through Coming Alongside

As the hurricane's winds and waves buffeted the listing *Wahine*, every attempt to get a line to her from one of the tugboats failed. Despite the extreme conditions the deputy harbormaster, Captain Galloway, attempted to clamber from one of the harbor tugboats onto a rope ladder hung over the side of the *Wahine*. To do this, he had to leap from the bow of the tugboat and grab the rope ladder, then quickly climb the 10.5 meters up the ladder to the deck. Captain Robertson believed Galloway would be crushed between the two ships, but Galloway managed to make it aboard the *Wahine*. Now one of the most experienced harbormasters was on board to help rescue ship and passengers.

Coming alongside people in the worst of storms is risky, sometimes scary, and always the sort of experience in which our own faith is challenged, stretched, tested, and seasoned. Captain Galloway had been on the tug all night; his shift was over. He had watched the wind and the waves snap a four-inch-thick tug cable like a piece of cotton. He knew the risks involved in climbing aboard a sinking ship. Still, he chose to come alongside and help.

When we have sailed through storms of our own, we may be trusted by God to come alongside others in their own storms. Being alongside does not mean captaining their ship. Each of our storms of faith and life is deeply personal. No two are the same, and no one can captain someone else's ship. One night, in a harbor overlooking the rocks struck by the *Wahine*, I came alongside a friend facing a very difficult storm of her own. It was a storm so painful, so encompassing, so dark, that my friend only wanted to climb the face of the cliff and throw herself into the sea. She asked to walk along the dark, unlit, rain-swept beach to the cliff face. I sensed that she needed to go, and that I had to go too. We walked side by side, the sea crashing on the rocks as the rain and wind drove into our backs. When we reached the cliff, we stopped and looked ahead, talked about choices, facing loneliness, and what had happened that brought her to this point of despair. I put my hand on her shoulder, wooing her to turn, to head away from the cliff. We were both scared and wet, and I was out of my depth. Slowly, she turned, and we walked into the wind back to the lights of the road.

Sometimes being seasoned means knowing only too well the limits of safety, yet finding ourselves called to go beyond safe practice. To do so is a dangerous choice, a risk-filled choice, yet one that a storm may demand. Sometimes we consciously step beyond safe practice at personal risk for the sake of another. We do so knowing that the responsibility of the choice we make is on our shoulders. It is a difficult seasoning.

## The Patron Saint of Seasoned Sailors

The patron saint of sailors is Saint Brendan the Navigator. Over fifteen hundred years ago, Brendan lived in a mountain monastery until he sensed a call to set sail for new lands to take the gospel. After fasting and praying for forty days, he stood on a beach of Southern Ireland looking out across the seas. In front of him stood a small boat. Leather skins smeared with animal fat stretched across a wooden frame. A flimsy craft for what would become for Brendan and his companions a seven-year journey from Ireland to Wales, Iona, Scotland, France, Iceland, Greenland, and possibly even America.

Imagine the fearful faith and the conflicted courage he felt as his craft began to "drift free at the mercy of wind and the whim of the waves—in the will of God." A prayer attributed to Brendan opens a window on his feelings:

> Shall I abandon, O King of mysteries, the soft comforts of home?
> Shall I turn my back on the native land, and turn my face towards the sea?
> Shall I put myself wholly at your mercy
> Without silver, without horse, without fame, without honor?
> Shall I throw myself wholly upon you, without sword and shield
> Without food and drink?
> Without a bed to lie on?
> Shall I say farewell to my beautiful land, placing myself under your yoke?
>
> Shall I pour out my heart to you, confessing my manifold sins and
> Begging forgiveness, tears streaming down my cheeks?
> Shall I leave the prints of my knees on the sandy beach?
> A record of my final prayer in my native land?
>
> Shall I then suffer every kind of wound that the sea can inflict?
> Shall I take my tiny boat across the wide sparkling ocean?

O king of the glorious heaven
Shall I go of my own choice upon the sea?[16]

Here the courage and commitment of following Christ into the storms are found. Put yourself in Saint Brendan's shoes. Imagine the knee prints on the beach are evidence of your final prayer before setting sail. Imagine you are the one standing on the edge of your known world, staring across the ocean to unknown horizons. Maybe there is something out there, maybe there isn't. Imagine stepping into the fragile boat of wood and leather smeared with animal fat to seal it from the waves.[17] What does it feel like to, like Saint Brendan, abandon the shore—leaving behind all models and strategies, ignoring old maps and guides, cut adrift from techniques and traditions, with your future solely in the hands of God?

How did Brendan navigate? Brendan is often depicted holding a paddle in one hand and a large Celtic cross in the other. Old burial sites indicate that Celtic crosses may have begun as a form of navigation—the first sextants. I am inspired by the notion of Saint Brendan navigating the calm seas and storms by way of the cross. The notion is not unfamiliar to those of us in the southern hemisphere, for whom the Southern Cross of the night sky is a common point of navigation.

## Preparing for the Perfect Storm

The crew of the *Wahine* kept the ship afloat for six hours as harbor tugs came to their aid. Eventually the order was given to abandon the listing ship. The crew got everyone off the ship alive, but the desperate sea conditions sadly meant many died before reaching land. Some of those in the water were picked up by the harbor tugs and brave boaties who had come out in the worst of conditions to save lives. But by the end of the day, fifty-one people had died. Some drowned. Some died of exposure in the freezing conditions. Others were dashed against the rocks by the powerful surf.

The storms approaching the church in Western contexts are real storms, dangerous storms. Storms in which we are endangered, and not all will end as happy tales of success. This is the reality of the church's history through periods of persecution, hardship, and struggle. And yet it is in such times that the Christian faith and church has grown.

When the perfect storm breaks, it will be too late to prepare—too late to consult manuals or ask for advice. It will be a time when only the experience, skill, and courage of seasoned sailors will do. So go on; set sail. Become a seasoned sailor. Where are you called to sail? What is your tide of obedience? How are you being prompted to move beyond present knowledge, experience, ideas, and securities? What does it mean for you to navigate your journey by the cross?

Sir Francis Drake set out from England in 1577 bound for America. Three years and thirty-six thousand miles later, at the perennial risk of their lives, he and his men had circumnavigated the globe. The following prayer is attributed to him:

> Disturb us, Lord when
> We are too well pleased with ourselves,
> When our dreams have come true
> Because we have dreamed too little,
> When we arrived safely
> Because we sailed too close to the shore.
> Disturb us, Lord when
> With the abundance of things we possess
> We have lost our thirst
> For the waters of life;
> Having fallen in love with life,
> We have ceased to dream of eternity
> And in our efforts to build a new earth,
> We have allowed our vision
> Of the new Heaven to dim.
> Disturb us, Lord, to dare more boldly,
> To venture on wider seas
> Where storms will show your mastery;
> Where losing sight of land,
> We shall find the stars.
> We ask you to push back
> The horizons of our hopes;
> And to push into the future
> In strength, courage, hope and love.[18]

## CHAPTER FIVE

# Exposing Our Murky Motives

DRIES LOMBAARD *(South Africa)*

*Make yourselves at home in My love.*
*If you'll keep My commands,*
*you'll remain intimately at home in My love.*
*But remember the root command:*
*Love one another.*

JOHN 15:9-10; 17 "THE MESSAGE"

## Christian Community as Anesthesia

Small groups have become an extension of most churches. They go by different names (for example, cell groups, small groups, care groups, house churches, fellowship, and so on), but they are now as prevalent in churches as worship services, evangelism, and youth programs.

What are the purposes of small groups? The right answer, which almost everyone gives you, is *community*. That's a no-brainer. The situation becomes more problematic when one asks for a definition or description of *community*. Some will refer to *community* as a place where people are polite, hospitable, and friendly. Others think of *community* as a place where people share their deepest struggles, triumphs, tears, and laughter. Should we be surprised by these multiple definitions? Not if we understand the trap of generalization.

Semantic generalization assumes that words carry the same meaning in different contexts. For example, we commit semantic generalization when we interpret the vocabulary of the biblical, Middle Eastern world according to the models, systems, and ideals of modernism. The theological terminology is the same in both worlds, but the theological understanding or experience is not. Semantic generalization is especially dangerous when it happens to terms that define the essence of God—terms like *grace*, *love*, *justice*, and *community*.

When the church generalizes semantically, we begin to accept our values as a given or a reality merely because we're using the correct terms. However, our terms don't correspond to their intended meanings and the values they represent. For example, using the term *community* may soothe us into believing that community is practiced authentically in our midst. The reality, however, is that we may have diluted the term to make it compatible with our very weak experience of the value it represents.

This is, in essence, why today's postmodern person is not satisfied by semantics. Postmoderns recognize that a single term cannot carry the full weight of its meaning in a given context. Therefore, a postmodern prefers pictures and images (which speak a thousand words) and, above all, *experiences*. You cannot semantically sell small groups to a perfect storm world. Postmoderns insist on an authentic experience of what you want them to believe.

Our murky motives have desensitized us to the real power of Christian community. The first church never *did* community; they *were* community. Just listen to the small-group language we use in church today: "We must *get* everyone in small groups." "Let people *do* life together." Then, we call the outcome *community*. I am not arguing against contextualization, but it sometimes seems as if the church reckons it can say something better than God has already said it. I am not against organization, but it sometimes seems as if the church believes it can create its own structures and the outcome will be authentic. We've swallowed the nominalist bait—hook, line, and sinker. We are so obsessed with slotting the value of community somewhere in our church activities that we never stop to think what the basic purpose of any small group should be—the *love* verb, not the *share* verb nor the *care* verb, neither the *teach* verb nor the *reach* verb. It is not about the *grow* verb or the *flow* verb. It is all about the *love* verb. Only this motive is adequate for the transformational expectations normative in the New Testament context.

Jesus taught his followers the practicality of love—he did not organize structures, set up timetables, appoint facilitators, and call it *community*. His motive was to model and teach love in action, to show it within his cultural context. His motive came from who he was—love. Because *love* is not a verb anymore today, we've chosen to verbalize it through structures. And it is exactly there that our motives become murky.

The only acceptable motive for small groups is *agape* love: unconditional love, with the understanding that such love can only exist, by definition, alongside imperfection. Where there is no sin, unconditional love is not needed. Therefore, we must be willing not only to accommodate and tolerate but also to love consistently. If we don't somehow see through Jesus' eyes of love, if respect isn't the innermost motive of our hearts, we'll keep on doing structural things as an anesthetic to the messiness of real love. We'll never move beyond the Wednesday evening, 7–9 P.M. culture of *feel-good caring and sharing*.

Following Christ is a journey. The destination has nothing to do with us. Jesus secured it. Our lives together as followers of Christ are all about the journey. It's not about measuring the times and distances of our individual journeys and comparing the states of our souls. In Christlike community, it's about pacing each other, not racing each other. Being the father of three small girls—the youngest still a baby of fourteen months—I'm amazed at how precisely we classify children in terms of their development and age. Friends of ours have a baby that is a mere six months older than our youngest. But they insist on calling ours the "baby" and theirs a "big girl." When we were teens, everyone in the group knew who was a single year older or younger than the others. As we grow older, it stretches to decades. Have you ever seen an eighty-two-year-old smiling at an eighty-one-year-old for still being a youngster? We mix with others in their thirties or forties seeing them as our peers. Go to a seniors' home and listen to a seventy-year-old and a ninety-year-old talk about the good old days. Now go to a kindergarten and listen to a three-year-old and four-year-old rival about who's the oldest. Maybe it's because early development accentuates change and growth. Perhaps the older we get, the less we expect change to occur regularly. We expect stability rather than change.

We tend to do exactly the same regarding Christian maturity. Our focus on the peripheral issues (who knows whatever, did whatever, and experienced whatever) overshadows the important central issue of journeying together. I've read that the aging Billy Graham and his ministry team all bought houses in the same neighborhood where they could retire. Asked why, they replied, "So we could see each other off into eternity." To me, that is mature, authentic community. That is Acts 2.

As the perfect storm exposes our murky motives, I hope it will also increase our capacity for astonishment and bewilderment in relationships. The fruit of the Spirit as listed in Galatians 5:22 is directly linked to how maturely we handle bewilderment. Most relationships are painfully damaged, sometimes even sunk, by our incapability to accommodate bewilderment within Christian community. We attack people who shock us with their beliefs, behavior, or sin; we accuse them of being phony and false; we label them Pharisees or deliberate frauds—all of this because we are emotionally incapable of handling disappointment. I've seen many small groups disintegrate because Christians couldn't deal with disappointment.

Want to experience community? Expect bewilderment. Expect disappointment. Expect sin. That is what the cross is all about: God expecting to be disappointed by our sin. The whole Old Testament is full of God being disappointed by sin. The whole Old Testament is also about God saying: "Once more." The mark of God's pain is the cross. It is the mark of grace. We should learn to cover each other—and ourselves—in God's grace. Murky motives erect high-jump poles in the midst of our communities, continually raise the bar, and ask, "Who's going to show us how?" Agape love replaces these poles with a cross, realizing that Christ showed us all how.

Let's see if the turbulent waves of the perfect storm will end the murkiness of terms like *small groups* and reveal the true meaning of the agape love of Christ. Paul wrote, "these three remain: faith, hope and love. But the greatest of these is love."[1] He was not philosophizing. He was not preaching. He was being acutely practical! To me it has always been significant that Paul followed the image of the church as a body in 1 Corinthians 12 with his elevation of love in 1 Corinthians 13; 1 Corinthians 13 is 1 Corinthians 12 coming into being.

*Jesus knew that the Father had put him in complete charge of everything, that he came from God and was on his way back to God. So he got up from the supper table, set aside his robe, and put on an apron. Then he poured water into a basin and began to wash the feet of the disciples, drying them with his apron.*

JOHN 13:3-5 "THE MESSAGE"

## The Self-serving Status Quo

The major blunder that church leaders make in getting people to serve is that they do not understand their own role in serving the servants. The existing structures of servanthood suggest that almost all leaders are utterly missing the mark in this respect. Perhaps the perfect storm will succeed where the Reformation failed to eliminate a professional class of ministers, ordained and paid to serve the laity. This hierarchical structure has divided the Body of Christ into two distinct groups: those who are called to do the work of ministry, and the rest who are called to support them in their work—either financially or physically. This divide has left some feeling inferior to minister and others feeling elevated to the task. Unknowingly, the authority has shifted from the holiness of the service to the holiness of the servant. Almost everyone seems to be biblically blind in this regard. I heard someone remark recently that, for the sake of the truth, we are keeping the lies intact. Most clergy have become addicted to being wanted and needed in ministry. Meanwhile, the strongest supporters of a professional ministry class are often the laity, who believe that ordaining and paying someone to pray, preach, and pastor relieves them of their own ministry responsibilities. The codependent relationship between clergy and laity is helpful to no one. To quote Christian Smith:

> The clergy-system is fundamentally self-defeating. Its stated purpose is to nurture spiritual maturity in the church—a valuable goal. In actuality, however, it accomplishes the opposite by nurturing a permanent dependence of the laity on the clergy. Clergy become to their congregations like parents whose children never grow up, like therapists whose clients never become healed, like teachers whose students never graduate. The existence of a full-time, professional minister makes it too easy for church members not to take responsibility for the ongoing life of the church. And why should they? That's the job of the pastor.[2]

Recently I once again heard a minister of a respected and renewal-oriented church within our denomination declare that "if something is biblical, we will support it with all our energy . . . and if something is unbiblical, we will reject it with all our energy." Sadly, he said this from an elevated pulpit, preaching as the ordained minister, oblivious to the very thing that he does not even see—as an ordained and professional minister, his very position is unbiblical.

What is the biblical responsibility of those who are called to give all their time into ministry? First, it is not wrong to be paid to do ministry—but monetary reward should never be the central focus. Second, it is not wrong to have certain responsibilities regarding ministry, but ordination is not found in the New Testament. (The same goes for being anointed.) Ordination—whether by heritage (for example, the Levites) or anointing (for example, David)—is replaced in the New Testament by vocation and giftedness. Paul, Timothy, and Peter, for example, were called and gifted. As the Holy Spirit is present within every believer, it is no longer necessary to have individuals anointed or ordained. It is truly a priesthood of all believers.

That the church fails to grasp this understanding of ministry is made more ironic by the fact that this understanding is not original to the New Testament! Moses already understood the essence of ministry by all for all. In Exodus 18, we read of the wise advice Moses received from his father-in-law, Jethro. After seeing Moses bogged down by the impossible task of managing all Israel's affairs, he spoke to Moses quite bluntly: "What's going on here? Why are you doing all this, and all by yourself, letting everybody line up before you from morning to night?"[3] The answer Moses gave is, to me, one of the classic revelations of an ordination mindset: "Because the people come to me with questions about God. When something comes up, they come to me. I judge between a man and his neighbor and teach them God's laws and instructions."[4]

Do you see the blame-shifting in his answer? "The people come to me," Moses says, as if he does not expect them to, as if he does not want them to. Jethro is not fooled:

> Moses' father-in-law said, "This is no way to go about it. You'll burn out, and the people right along with you. This is way too much for you—you can't do this alone. Now listen to me. Let me tell you how to do this so that God will be in this with you. Be there for the people before God, but let the matters of concern be presented to God. Your job is to teach them the rules and instructions, to show them how to live, what to do. And then you need to keep a sharp eye out for competent men—men who fear God, men of integrity, men who are incorruptible—and appoint them as leaders over groups organized by the thousand, by the hundred, by fifty, and by ten. They'll be responsible for the everyday work of judging among the people. They'll bring the hard cases to you, but in the routine cases they'll be the judges. They will share your load and that will make it easier for you. If you handle the work this way, you'll have the strength to carry out whatever God commands you, and the people in their settings will flourish also."[5]

Jethro acknowledged that Moses had the authority and wisdom and stature to handle the hard cases, but he also taught him the most basic lesson in leadership: build teams.

You might argue that this proves nothing: Moses is still singularly ordained by God for this work of ministry. True, but not for long. Jump to Numbers 11, where Moses is in the midst of a pity party because of all his responsibilities. God feels sorry for him and decides to help him out:

> God said to Moses, "Gather together seventy men from among the leaders of Israel, men whom you know to be respected and responsible. Take

> them to the Tent of Meeting. I'll meet you there. I'll come down and speak with you. I'll take some of the Spirit that is on you and place it on them; they'll then be able to take some of the load of this people—you won't have to carry the whole thing alone."[6]

What happens here? History changes: Moses, the first man to receive the Holy Spirit for ministry is now being multiplied by God, by the giving of the Holy Spirit to seventy more men.

> So Moses went out and told the people what God had said. He called together seventy of the leaders and had them stand around the Tent. God came down in a cloud and spoke to Moses and took some of the Spirit that was on him and put it on the seventy leaders. When the Spirit rested on them they prophesied. But they didn't continue; it was a onetime event.[7]

Was this the end of Holy Spirit–endowed ministry? Not for all. It seemed that two men loved it too much to stop:

> Meanwhile two men, Eldad and Medad, had stayed in the camp. They were listed as leaders but they didn't leave camp to go to the Tent. Still, the Spirit also rested on them and they prophesied in the camp.[8]

Oops. They're doing ministry amongst the people, without the proper ordination! The first special aggrieved church board meeting was called:

> A young man ran and told Moses, "Eldad and Medad are prophesying in the camp!" Joshua son of Nun, who had been Moses' right-hand man since his youth, said, "Moses, master! Stop them!"[9]

Joshua, of all people—Moses' second-in-command—could not take this. *Who gave them the right? Who ordained them? They never even went to seminary!* Then, the wisest words I think Moses ever spoke:

> But Moses said, "Are you jealous for me? Would that all God's people were prophets. Would that God would put his Spirit on all of them."[10]

If only more pastors and ministers had this wisdom and insight. Ultimately, Moses' wish for a nation of prophets came true. We read about it in Acts 2. And this is what the "fivefold ministry" in Ephesians 4 is all about—not ordained positions, but gifts. These gifts enable some to become apostles, prophets, evangelists, shepherds (pastors), and teachers for a single, clear purpose: "to equip the saints for the work of ministry."[11] The gifts are never given, so a gifted few do all of the ministry and are supported by those who do none of the ministry. The gifted never claim to be more spiritual, more Godly or even more called. They have the roles of coaches, trainers, and supporters.

Ministers should once again become servants, after the model of Christ himself. I believe his act of washing the disciples' feet is much more than a symbolic act of servanthood. I believe he gave all of us the only model for ministry that will survive the perfect storm: *equipping through serving*. Look at the events unfolding in John 13:

> Just before the Passover Feast, Jesus knew that the time had come to leave this world to go to the Father. Having loved his dear companions, he continued to love them right to the end. It was suppertime. The Devil by now had Judas, son of Simon the Iscariot, firmly in his grip, all set for the betrayal.
>
> Jesus knew that the Father had put him in complete charge of everything, that he came from God and was on his way back to God. So he got up from the supper table, set aside his robe, and put on an apron. Then he poured water into a basin and began to wash the feet of the disciples, drying them with his apron.[12]

There are two distinct statements that we should not miss. The first is the statement "Having loved his dear companions, he continued to love them right to the end."[13] We're back to the basics. You cannot serve people if you do not love them. Second, the statement, "Jesus knew that the Father had put him in complete charge of everything, that he came from God and was on his way back to God."[14] Get it? You cannot serve people if you are not absolutely sure of your authority, where you come from, and where you are going. This one sentence tells us that Jesus was absolutely secure about who he was, about his mission, and about his destiny. Combine this with honest love for the people you serve, and you create an authentic disciple-making ministry—no murky motives, no self-serving hierarchies, only a church of disciples, prepared to weather the perfect storm.

CHAPTER SIX

# Reorienting the Church of the Twenty-first Century

YOUNGLAE KIM *(South Korea)*

In the modern era, the church needed a Re*formation*. In a postmodern, post-Christendom era, Leonard Sweet believes the church needs a Re*orientation*.[1] *Orient* literally means "east." Therefore, to reorient the church means to point it toward the East—to the churches of Asia—in hopes of freeing its ecclesiology, soteriology, Christology, and so on from Western captivity. In reference to the future of Christianity, Pope John Paul II used the metaphor of a body with two lungs: an Eastern lung and a Western lung. If Christianity has been breathing only with the left lung of Western culture (rational, scientific, analytic), it is time to breathe also with the right lung of Eastern culture (affective, spiritual, holistic). The church of the third millennium must breathe with *both lungs*.[2]

What is going on in the churches of the East, and Korean churches in particular? Korean churches have little more than one hundred years of history but have achieved remarkable growth in numbers and strength. Korean megachurches have redefined *mega*, varying in size from over seven thousand to even one hundred thousand members. Without a doubt, the current success of Korean Protestantism has to do with the fervent missionary endeavor of Western churches at the turn of the twentieth century. To abbreviate a very long and complex story, I've simplified the evolution of Korean churches with three characteristic phases:[3]

1. Personal/social salvation evangelism (1885–1995)
2. Seeker-friendly ministry (1995–2005)
3. Mission rediscovery church (2005 and beyond)

Implanted by USAmerican missionaries and led by Korean proponents of democratization, the emphasis on evangelism drove the growth of Korean churches until the late twentieth century. As in USAmerica, there was conflict between the personal gospel and social gospel groups, but both sides worked for salvation (in different ways). In terms of church size, the personal gospel emphasis was more successful than the emphasis on a social gospel. However, signs of membership decline appeared in many Korean churches by the last quarter of the twentieth century. Korean churches began looking at seeker-friendly USAmerican churches for inspiration—ranging from the Crystal Cathedral to nontraditional churches such as Saddleback Church and Willow Creek Community Church. The outcome was that big churches got bigger and small churches got smaller. The so-called Wal-Martization of the church that marked the religious scene in the United States happened in Korea as well.

What does the future hold for Korean churches? I am hoping for a mission rediscovery church. The Great Commission[4] suggests that mission is the maker and marker of the genuine church. Missional churches are now arriving on the Korean scene, although there is a long way to go before this becomes the dominant theme or thrust. I am not arguing that personal/social salvation evangelism or seeker-friendly ministry must be thrown overboard. Rather, my hope is that what I am calling the mission rediscovery church will become a milestone for Western and Eastern churches looking for a twenty-first-century reorientation.

What makes the mission rediscovery church different from churches that emphasize personal/social salvation evangelism or seeker-friendly ministry? It's the direction by which the church is guided in its goings and its comings. I hope to elaborate more about this in subsequent writings. In this article, I would like to deal with three driving forces, which are very much Korean and yet still valid for the integrity of the church in general. I shall also propose a direction for the mission rediscovery church and frame it in terms of an emerging feature of Korean churches, in the hope that it might set the churches of tomorrow on the path of reorientation.

## Spiritual CPR: Reviving the Church

Breathing is a critical activity of the human body. When a person is unconscious and his or her breathing and pulse cannot be detected, an emergency first aid protocol known as cardiopulmonary resuscitation (CPR) is administered. The body is a biblical metaphor for the church. Thus, when the church loses its vital signs, its revival depends on spiritual CPR.

Spiritual CPR consists of three practices: congregating (C), praying (P), and reading the Bible (R). Korean churches have not only learned this emergency treatment but also kept it from losing its vitality over time. The story goes back to 1907, a year that bears a significant historical meaning for Korean churches. In January 1907, a Bible study convention was held at Jandaehyun Church in Pyoungyang. Later it would be called the Korean Pentecost by church historians.[5] At least fifteen hundred people gathered at the convention to hear preachers such as Sun Joo Gil encourage them to read their Bibles, confess their sins, and experience spiritual transformation. After closing the convention on January 14, five hundred to six hundred people remained to pray. They prayed all night until 10 A.M. the next day, all the while experiencing the power of the Holy Spirit. From that moment forward, *Saebyuk Gidohoe* (early-morning prayer meeting) *Chulya Gidohoe* (overnight prayer meeting), *Tongsung Gido* (praying out loud in unison), and Bible study convention, along with *Bible Tongdok* (reading through the Bible), have become the indigenous hallmarks of Korean Christianity.[6]

How is spiritual CPR practiced in Korean churches today?

## Congregating (*Saebyuk Gidohoe/Chulya Gidohoe*)

Every church has *Saebyuk Gidohoe* (early-morning prayer meeting) in the rural regions from 4:00 A.M. or 4:30 A.M. or in the cities from 4:30 A.M. to 5:00 A.M. Most churches also offer *Chulya Gidohoe* (overnight prayer meeting) beginning Friday at 10 P.M. and continuing until the Saturday morning prayer meeting. These meetings usually do not have a closing time and go on until the last participant leaves the meeting place. These two kinds of prayer meetings are based on two biblical texts: "Very early in the morning, while it was still dark, Jesus got up, left the house and went off to a solitary place, where he prayed,"[7] and "Jesus went to the mountains and all through the night he prayed to God."[8]

## Praying (*Tongsung Gido*)

*Tongsung Gido* means praying aloud and usually loudly. As members of the congregation simultaneously engage in earnest petition, prayer becomes both personal and communal.[9] In the Scripture, there are many verbs used for prayer that entail shouting or crying out. In Hebrew, there are about ten different root words that mean crying out in a loud voice: the Israelites perceived crying out to God in more differentiated fashion than do most Christians today.

## Reading the Bible (*Bible Tongdok*)

*Bible Tongdok* (reading the Bible) encourages learners to read a text or a classic over and over again until they gain a perspective, grasp a big picture, and finally reach an intuition. *Bible Tongdok* also means one reads "the entire Bible through from the top to the bottom regarding sixty-six books as one book and not as parts but as a whole."[10] In other words, the purpose of reading the entire Bible is to understand passages within the context of the whole Word of God, keeping in mind that "All Scripture is God-breathed and is useful for teaching, rebuking, correcting and training in righteousness, so that the man of God may be thoroughly equipped for every good work."[11]

## *Waking Up the* Holon *World*

One of the major church-supported newspapers in Korea featured an article, "Early Morning Prayer Meeting, Wake Up the Whole World" on February 25, 2006.[12] The article reports, "*Saebyuk Gidohoe* is being revived again. . . . It, one of the prideful programs of Korean churches, is being rediscovered as a keyword for the church revival of twenty-first century."[13] A month earlier, another newspaper dealt with the history of this unique Korean church tradition under the title of "Again 1907."

Why the reference to 1907? Until 1907, Western missionaries sowed the seeds of the gospel in Korea. In 1907, Korean Christians assumed the task and brought an Eastern perspective to Western Christianity. They recalled the words of Jesus, who told his disciples to stay in Jerusalem and wait for the Holy Spirit. Accordingly, they prayed and experienced the Word of God by listening to the Scriptures and sharing their personal relationship with Jesus Christ. In essence, what they did was put their understanding (mind) and experience (heart) together. In so doing, they realized the power of holarchy.

Holarchy is "the order (arche) of *holons* (whole/parts)."[14] Spatial and temporal parts and the whole have been merged and mingled in the concept of *holon*. Often we make a mistake in terms of seeing the trees and not seeing the forest. Leonard Sweet, Brian McLaren, and Jerry Haselmayer say,

> All quantum systems exhibit the double ring. Matter is both wave and particle. Similarly, humans have a particle component (individual) and a wave component (cultural/communal). We are both self and community, both core and periphery. Holons contain both self-preservation (particle) and self-adaptation (wave).[15]

Spiritual CPR promotes holarchy. *Saebyuk Gidohoe* and *Chulya Gidohoe* (congregating) go beyond the limit of time and space in gathering; *Tongsung Gido* (praying) also shows that there is no distinction between individuality and collectivity; and *Tongdok* (reading) makes it possible to see the parts and the whole of Scripture at the same time.

Although it's a truism to say that a church in Korea wouldn't be considered much of a church if it doesn't practice spiritual CPR, a question remains: why doesn't spiritual CPR work for every Korean church? The answer lies in seeing spiritual CPR not as a program but as a power conduit. Spiritual CPR becomes powerful only when it brings opposites together—time/timelessness, space/spacelessness, individuals/community, parts/whole. The church needs to understand the paradoxical nature of truth in Christian faith. By virtue of its Eastern mind-set, the Korean church is well-poised to embrace the power of paradoxy.

*Almost every wise saying has an opposite one, no less wise, to balance it.*

GEORGE SANTAYANA[16]

*The opposite of a correct statement is a false statement. But the opposite of a profound truth may well be another profound truth.*

NIELS BOHR[17]

*The sane person . . . always cares more for truth than consistency. If he sees two truths that seem to contradict each other, he accepts both truths and the contradiction along with them. His intellectual sight is stereoscopic, like his physical sight: he sees two different pictures at once and yet sees all the better for that.*

G. K. CHESTERTON[18]

Forget about logical consistency. Let the Holy Spirit be in charge of the church.

## Alternating Current

As Korean churches lead the reorientation of the twenty-first-century church, we need to ask, "What are we going to do with spiritual CPR power?"

> I tell you the truth, unless a kernel of wheat falls to the ground and dies, it remains only a single seed. But if it dies, it produces many seeds. The man who loves his life will lose it, while the man who hates his life in this world will keep it for eternal life.[19]

In the evangelism period of Korean church history, personal and social salvation was the goal. In more recent times, seeker-friendly ministry has produced the largest megachurches in the world. Yet we know from past experience that power cannot flow inward indefinitely. That's why a new, emerging trend of the church is needed: the mission rediscovery church. If Korean churches can realize the dream of a mission rediscovery church, they can lead the way for churches around the world.

The twenty-first-century church needs to run on AC (alternating current). Spiritual power must flow in two directions: in and out, out and in. In the New Testament writings, the church is called an *ekklesia*, which is a combination of *ek*, "out of," and *kalein*, "to call." The church is always gathering and scattering its people. The church is not only God's fortress but also God's force. The spiritual power that attracts large numbers of people into church must be used to send them out from church. It's not easy for institutionalized and organized churches to run on alternating current. Nevertheless, we must do it.

## Emerging Churches in Korea

*In/Out: Se-Shin Methodist Church (www.seshin.org)*

Se-Shin Methodist Church is a typical midsize church in Seoul, Korea, with two thousand adult members and one thousand children. This church recently captured the attention of Holt A. Clarke, the author of *Created for God's Mission: Fashioning a Great Commission Church for a 21st Century World?*[20] Reverend Jong Soo Kim founded the church in March 1978 with his wife, Chun Sil Kang. Since the church's inception, Pastor Kim has defined the Se-Shin Church as "participatory mission." The church has planted *over forty* churches in southwestern Asia, resulting in more than 120 local ministry units (one church normally supports three to four groups).[21] Building a church costs from ten thousand to fifteen thousand dollars, depending on the location. Pastor Kim encourages a family to participate in this church-planting mission by building a church dedicated in their name. When the construction of a church is completed, the family goes on a mission trip to be part of the dedication service. Through this hands-on experience of mission, the family becomes permanent supporters of the church in the mission field. Se-Shin Church is not a megachurch in the Korean standard of church membership, but the mega scale of the church's mission deserves to be celebrated.[22]

Pastor Kim makes it clear that the church is not interested in attraction ministries but devotes itself solely to domestic and world mission. The church wants to be a mission rediscovery church—nothing else. The power coming into the church through spiritual CPR pushes the church back outside, to the ends of the world. Every aspect of the church's ministry focuses on world mission. Even the class names for Sunday school are taken from the names of mission fields such as China, Cuba, Nepal, Tanzania, Bulgaria, and so on. The church advocates "missional living," that is "a commonality displayed in emergent churches . . . the belief that all believers are active missionaries of Christ in their daily lives."[23]

*Out/In: Hanshi Mission (www.hanshi.or.kr)*

Hanshi Mission started as a campus ministry. It was founded by Dr. Byungho Zoh in 1988 and is well-known for Supgwanamu School for *Bible Tongdok* and *Purigisayuk/Muljugisayuk*. The Hanshi Mission began with *Purigisayuk/Muljugisayuk*, created to serve less-fortunate neighbors living in remote locations. In 1989, Hanshi Mission started the *Bible Tongdok* Camp, which trains youth, young adults, laity, and clergy to read the Bible from a forest and trees perspective. And in 2004, Dr. Zoh founded Higippum Church, with three ministry themes: Bible, history, and practice. The church worships on Sundays at a high school auditorium and holds weekday meetings at Dahaewon, a futuristic complex with a book café, conference rooms, lecture halls, and offices.

Recently, Dr. Zoh presented a motto for his ministry: "Let's Tong!" This motto encourages people to bring opposites together, gain an organic perspective, and do real things in any/certain time and any/certain space. His conviction arose from nineteen years of reading through the Bible (*Tongdok*). His reading always comes with prayer and becomes a source of power to transform the lives of individuals and communities.

Dr. Zoh's lifetime commitment to "love the neighbors" through domestic mission and "feel the heart of God" through reading through the Bible make his ministry distinct in terms of overcoming the dichotomy between I and Thou and mind and heart.[24] His Forest and Tree, International Method of reading through the Bible is going beyond national boundaries to share the joy of service and the excitement of learning with people of all nations.

Together, Hanshi Mission and Higippum Church are an out-in (and out again) ministry: they scatter to gather, then scatter again. Through books, forums, campus network, web, and media, Dr. Zoh is creating a multifaceted mission. The work of this ministry cannot be measured by the size of the building or the number of its membership.

## Be Creative! Be Courageous!

The church is revived by spiritual CPR, the source of its creative power. Once the power is on, the church must be courageous enough to let it flow in both directions: in and out, out and in. The twenty-first-century church needs to be creative and courageous to keep in step with the always-advancing kingdom of God:

Be Creative! Get the power from spiritual CPR:

- Congregate anytime and anyplace, online or off-line, small or large
- Pray individually or communally, silently or vocally, with words or with images
- Read through the Bible partially and wholly, praying with and praying through

> Do not leave Jerusalem, but wait for the gift my Father promised, which you have heard me speak about. . . . But you will receive power when the Holy Spirit comes on you; and you will be my witnesses in Jerusalem, and in all Judea and Samaria, and to the ends of the earth.[25]

Be Courageous! Let the power flow in both directions.
In/Out.
Out/In.

Therefore, go and make disciples of all nations, baptizing them in the name of the Father and of the Son and of the Holy Spirit, and teaching them to obey everything I have commanded you. And surely I am with you always, to the very end of the age. [26]

CHAPTER SEVEN

# The Perfect Storm as a Paradigmic Theory

EARL J. PIERCE *(United States)*

## The Power of Paradigms

Since the middle of the last century, there has been an increasing interest in the theory of paradigms as a means of explaining scientific and social progress. Beginning with Kenneth Boulding's *Image* (1956), which explored how we understand and interact with the world around us, to the classic *The Structure of Scientific Revolutions* (Kuhn, 1962), much has been written on the concept of paradigm as a means of explaining how we learn, understand, and make decisions. Joel Barker brought the concept to the masses in his 1993 video and book, *Paradigms: The Business of Discovering the Future.*

Paradigms are mental constructs—frameworks for understanding and answering the questions posed by the task at hand, be it scientific, social, or religious. Paradigms are built through experience: mental frameworks are developed so that answers can be postulated to questions without the experience having to be repeated. As long as a paradigm provides answers and progress continues, the paradigm is valued and remains in use by the individual or the group that developed it. Once a paradigm fails to produce useful solutions to the problems faced, it is abandoned. According to Barker, new paradigms often arise before old paradigms are played out. When a new paradigm begins to answer questions that an old paradigm can no longer answer, a paradigm shift occurs, and the old paradigm is consigned to history. When a paradigm shift occurs, all inquirers are returned to a common base, ground zero, as it were, and there is no competitive advantage based on prior experience or position.

Whereas paradigmic theory has been used in many settings, I would like to suggest the use of paradigms as a means of understanding the shift from the modern to the so-called postmodern, or emerging, culture. Using multiple paradigms to understand the history of Western culture, and the Christian church within that culture, might help Christian leaders understand the issues brought to the fore by emerging culture.

*God's Spirit brooded like a bird*
*above the watery abyss.*
GENESIS 1:2 "THE MESSAGE"

## The Metaphor of the Sea

In the past few years, images of the sea have been used to describe the enormity of the changes occurring locally and on a global scale. Terms such as *sea change* and *tsunami* and *aquachurch* have been popularized in this respect. I will continue this practice, using the term *perfect storm*, originally coined in 1991 to describe an enormous extratropical low that wrought major devastation along the New England coast. The sinking of the boat *Andrea Gail* in this perfect storm led to the book and motion picture of the same name. Because a perfect storm is such a vivid demonstration of the power of the wind and sea, the image is helpful in describing the forces that are affecting Christian congregations and denominations today.

The perfect storm was a natural phenomenon—a combination of naturally-occurring events resulting in something quite out of the ordinary, but natural nonetheless. From a purely scientific point of view, the storm was caused by the sun heating and cooling the earth and sea at different rates. This caused the air above both to rise and fall in relation to the temperature differences. This rising and falling caused the air also to move from warm (high pressure) to cold (low pressure) causing winds. The stronger the difference in temperature and pressure, the stronger the winds became. The wind moving over the water caused the water to develop waves in what is called the *fetch*. The longer the fetch, the larger the waves became. A perfect storm was born.

Christians believe that God is at work in the wind and the waves. The above quote from Genesis describes what could be called history's first wave: the Spirit (breath, wind) of God moved, hovered, fluttered, over the face of the deep. As we consider the piling up of paradigms at this moment in history, we can view them as waves, coming in and building up from all directions. In so doing, we have to keep before us the image of the Spirit of God hovering over the deep. It is God's world, God's creation, and God's waves that are coming together at this time.

God's hand is at work in the changes going on around us. How is God calling the church to respond? We cannot assume that there is only one answer to that question. Too often the church seeks a quick and easy answer to the problems it faces. Many are all too willing to offer the next big thing to solve them all. Unfortunately, as one issue is resolved, another rises to take its place. Much is done with a leaky boat: we try to get by with patches rather than bring the boat into dry dock and do the job right so that the ship can safely return to the sea.

This essay provides no quick fixes. It probably will not solve any problems at all. Its purpose is to help the church see the perfect storm in which we find ourselves and, in doing so, understand the many forces coming together to keep us in the harbor. The mission of the church is to go, not remain in the safety of the harbor. We are to go out to seek and save the lost. The unofficial motto of the U. S. Coast Guard is *we have to go out, but we don't have to come back*. Shouldn't this apply to the church as well?

## The Paradigm Shift from Cognitive to Affective

Psychology has long understood the two primary domains of human behavior as affective and cognitive. Emotion (affection) and reason (cognition) wage an ongoing duel for dominance of the individual.

Psychologists and other mental health professionals seek to assist the individual in finding a healthy balance, or tension, between the two.

I would suggest that the affective and cognitive domains be seen as two frameworks, or paradigms, for understanding the development of Western, Christendom culture. Kirk and Spock from the old *Star Trek* series would be good examples of persons working out of each paradigm, with Kirk the representative of the affective and Spock the cognitive. In an affective paradigm, answers based on feeling and emotion are controlling factors. How does it make me feel? Does the solution proposed by the affective paradigm help me feel better about myself or my circumstances? On the other hand, a cognitive paradigm seeks solutions based on reason and logic.

Christianity was born in the midst of the Greco-Roman cognitive paradigm, which had replaced an earlier affective paradigm. The cognitive paradigm provided answers in philosophy and the practical sciences that allowed these civilizations to develop into world powers. And yet, by the time of Christ, this paradigm was beginning to wear thin. The emperor cult and continuing militarism were not able to meet a developing thirst for the deeper things of life. Western culture was ready for a paradigm shift. Even while the cognitive paradigm continued its dominance, other, affective paradigms were beginning to make inroads in the culture. By the time Christianity began to move out of its Palestinian homeland, several paradigms were competing. Paul expresses this diversity of paradigms this way: "Jews demand miraculous signs and Greeks look for wisdom, but we preach Christ crucified: a stumbling block to Jews and foolishness to Gentiles."[1]

An interesting sidebar: in Judaism the religious leader is called *rabbi*, teacher, as opposed to the common Christian use of *pastor*, shepherd. Can we see, even here in the titles, the shift from cognition to affect?

Christianity won out in the empire not only because of its message but also because of the way this message embodied a new paradigm—an affective paradigm. Faith rather than logic, or reason, became the standard of living. The author of the letter to the Hebrews explains it thus: "Now faith is being sure of what we hope for and certain of what we do not see."[2] Only an affective paradigm would allow for this kind of certainty, a certainty not based on logic or facts.

This is not to say that the older paradigm no longer existed, only that its influence had become secondary to the new, affective paradigm. The cognitive paradigm still expressed itself in government and to some extent was adapted by the church as it assumed the role of government with the collapse of the Roman Empire. As more extreme affective paradigms (for example, Gnosticism) pressed forward, the majority in the church allowed the solutions proposed by cognition to moderate the effects of the affective.

The affective paradigm was dominant until the next shift began in the fourteenth century. Effects of this dominance can be seen in the rise of hereditary nobility based, not on reason or logic, but power and economics. Likewise, control in the church depended on emotion laced with the threat of the law. Scholasticism in the 1400s marks the return to dominance of the cognitive paradigm. This shift is commonly known as the beginning of the modern era. The development of the printing press and the full blossoming of the Renaissance released the cognitive paradigm throughout Europe. The power of this paradigm can be seen in how rapidly change occurred in all fields as a result.

The church was not immune to this shift. In fact, the Protestant reformation is a direct result of this shift, as is the emergence of denominationalism, which was formulated at the Westminster Assembly of Divines (1643). Because of the improvements in communications, this paradigm shift spread farther and faster than prior shifts and was able to push the envelope of its own existence farther than had been possible with the prior shift from cognitive to affective. Luther, for one, saw limits needed on this paradigm. Even though he was willing to use it to explore his faith and relationship with God, he was not willing to allow it to overrule what he saw as the absolutes or unknowables of faith.

In Lutheran theology, this is known as the magisterial versus the ministerial uses of reason. One example can be found in the only meeting of Luther and another noted Reformer, Zwingli, at the Marburg Colloquy of 1529. The issue was the word "is" in the verse, "Take; eat; this is my body."[3] Luther was unwilling to allow reason to overrule the text while Zwingli, coming at full force with the cognitive paradigm, could not allow for such an unreasonable solution.

Protestantism and modernity walked hand-in-hand under the cognitive paradigm. Whereas modernity has outpaced Protestantism in many ways (for example, the Enlightenment), many within the Protestant movement have sought to keep pace, leading to what is called mainline liberal Protestantism in the United States.

Again, this is not to say that the affective paradigm ceased to exert influence. A paradigm's power ebbs and flows. Each solution brings reaction, and each reaction demands yet another resolution. The rise of rationalism and pietism in the eighteenth century shows the tension that always exists within the dominant paradigm. When that paradigm can no longer provide answers, the shift begins.

## The Postmodern Paradigm Shift

Today, a shift is beginning once again from cognitive to affective. Can the Christianity that began with the Reformation return to its earlier, affective roots? And what will temper the rush to pure affect? Is there something unseen on the horizon that will provide that buffer?

Looking at the microlevel, we can ask how the swing from affective to cognitive works itself out within congregations. More often than not, a person begins attending a church because of an unmet need or through a relationship. In either case, it is the affective, not the cognitive, that is the causative agent behind the move. That is to say, the reasons a person explores the Christian faith are affective in nature. Once the person has made the decision to join, the congregation usually builds the person in his or her faith through the cognitive paradigm; that is, catechumens are taught the right things, the right doctrine, the right actions, assuming that it is through thinking that the person will continue to grow in her or his faith.

Yet it was not through thinking that the person was brought to faith in the first place. Without the reinforcement of the affective domain—without growing and multiplying relationships, without experiences in the congregation that meet the affective needs—the person will pull away, and often, in time, seek other means to have those needs met.

It is interesting to note that the modern era marked the rapid growth and influence of Western culture. The power shifted to countries that experienced a paradigm shift from the affective to the cognitive. The worldwide influence of Western culture flows from this cognitive influence as world leaders continued to move away from the Near

Eastern roots, from south and central Europe to England and the United States.

A final observation about paradigmic theory concerns the recent growth of both the Roman Catholic Church and the Orthodox churches. Neither fully adopted the new cognitive paradigm; by and large, both continued with the affective paradigm through the Reformation era to this day. Could this be the reason for their current appeal? And could this explain the greatest success story in Christian history: the hundred-year history of Pentecostalism?

Whereas the crest of the affective wave paradigm is fast approaching, the ebb of the cognitive still has to be considered as we face the future. And this paradigm shift is just one of many that are overlapping in the perfect storm. The church may ride through one wave only to find several others just as high and potentially destructive. The perfect storm is not just one paradigm shift but a multitude that combine to challenge the church to hold fast to the mast, the cross of Jesus Christ.

# CHAPTER EIGHT

# Mid-storm Equations for the Emerging Church

BILL EASUM *(United States)*

Big game fishing is one of the loves of my life. I live to be on the water, catch a billfish, and then release it to go on its way. When I'm on the water, I'm as close to heaven as I can get on this earth. That is as long as the water isn't disturbed by a storm. When a storm comes, everything on the water changes in a very short period of time. I've seen perfectly calm water become a raging nightmare in fewer than ten minutes, and heaven becomes a hell on earth. When that happens you have only one option—head into the storm. If you turn tail and try to outrun it, you could be swamped.

Ministry in today's emerging world is much the same. Effective leaders don't try to avoid the storms of life; instead, they risk everything and head straight into the storm. And believe me, those who are doing effective ministry today deal with one storm after another, because that's the nature of the emerging world.

We're living in a world in which most of the rules have changed. It may be fair to say that our world is without rules at the moment—that we are in between rules. As we plunge headlong away from the age of modernity into whatever we will call the emerging world, we're leaving behind most of the rules by which the game of life has been played. For instance, for several centuries Newtonian physics determined the basis for all scientific investigation, which implied a mechanical view of existence. Then along came quantum physics and all the rules of scientific investigation were called into question, and a more organic worldview was rediscovered. What quantum physics means to the emerging world is still being debated. But one thing is sure—Newtonian physics is not the final word on how to view existence. We are now in between rules, and the world is being viewed more organically than mechanically.

I'm probably older than the other contributors to this book. I was born in 1939 squarely in the heart of modernity. Most of you weren't even a gleam in your mother's eye then, and neither was the term *postmodern*. Today, most of the rules of the world into which I was born are either totally gone or dramatically altered.

The rules started changing slowly and incrementally early in my ministry. Over the last few decades, the slow, incremental changes have given way to a flood of fast-moving, exponential changes, causing a radical discontinuity in the world. Very little of what I grew up with has much meaning today when it comes to ministry. Only one thing hasn't changed—Jesus is the same yesterday, today, and forever. (I read that somewhere.)

So I've been saying for some time now our world is in between rules, and new rules will not emerge overnight. In the meantime, ministry must go on and people must find God. So I've played around with some mid-storm equations that might help us effectively and faithfully move from Modernity into the storm of the emerging world. These equations are not finished nor perfected—only emerging. Perhaps, when you finish reading this, you might want to add some more equations. If so, e-mail them to me at Easum@aol.com, and I'll put them on our website.

## Mid-storm Equations for Ministry

A new crop of leaders is emerging and they are teaching us a new set of equations by which to evaluate how we think and act. These new equations provide us with some hint of what lies ahead for the church.

### *Fractals Are the Guiding Principle of Mathematics in the Emerging World*

Fractalling is the constant repetition of something. A fractal is also any pattern that reveals greater complexity as it is enlarged. Take a look at the leaf. If you put a microscope on it you would see the constant

repetition of the vein system over and over. The twenty-first-century church will look more like a fractal than an institution and will look more organic than institutional.

Most of the math you studied in school is old knowledge. For example, the geometry you studied about circles, squares, and triangles was organized around 300 B.C. by a man named Euclid. Much of fractal geometry, however, is much newer. The word *fractal* was coined less than two decades ago.

What's the difference between Euclidian geometry and fractals? The more you magnify a circle or square or triangle, the simpler, clearer, and straighter the lines become. That's not true with fractals. The more you magnify a fractal, the more complicated the figure becomes and the more details you see.

So what have fractals to do with the church of the future? Everything. The emerging church will be far more diverse than most people think. Numerous books have been written lately on the emerging church. Many of these books are excellent in their content and analysis of the culture, but they seem to be too monolithic in their conclusions about the shape of the future church. Much of the writing today about the emerging church is still under the influence of Euclidian geometry and modernity and fails to see the implications of fractals. For all of the talk about the emerging church, or the organic church, or the fluid church, or the emergent church, authors seem to be making the assumption that there will be one dominant form of church in the future. I don't think so.

Although no one knows for sure what the church of the twenty-first century will look like, it's safe to say that it will not be the bland, one-style-fits-all church of modernity. The closer I look at what is happening today with the church, the more diverse and complicated the scene becomes. I don't see anything even close to a dominant form of church life. Instead, *at the moment*, I see five major forms of church life emerging. Each of these forms is carving out a larger niche of the church scene, but still only a niche.

I see islands of strength within the mainline denominations. On the other hand, I see numerous forms of marketplace congregations that have no institutional form whatsoever. In addition, I see a smaller, less institutionally based, emergent church that is more ancient/future. Next, I see the house church becoming more organized than ever before. Finally, I see the continuation of the high-commitment, disciple-making, culturally indigenous, megacongregation.

The emerging church is taking many forms, and the closer you examine them, the more types and shapes you begin to see. No one form of church will dominate the emerging world like it did in modernity. If we have learned anything about what may come after modernity for the church, it is that it will not be the one-size-fits-all world in which most of us have grown up.

Based on this first mid-storm equation, several more equations come to mind. Using them will determine the shape of your church in the twenty-first century.

### *Fractals, Multiplied by Themselves, Minus Addition or Subtraction, Equals the Church of the Twenty-first Century*

Whatever shape the twenty-first century church takes it will resemble more of an organic than institutional form. I expect to see the multisite movement become more of a norm than it is today. I expect to see the house-church movement continue to escalate. And I expect to see more churches focusing on multiple forms of church-planting than in the history of Christianity.

The key to understanding the twenty-first-century church will be to see it as an organic movement, and if that is so, then the stand-alone, institutionally based church will become a small niche rather than the norm. It won't go away—it will just no longer be the kind of church you think of when you hear the word *church*. When you invite someone to your church, one of the things you will have to decide is which of the branches of your church you are inviting this person to attend.

This form of church will resemble the church of Acts more than what we have seen since the fourth century. In a way, I am predicting a return to a more biblical form of the church—a present form of fractalling and multiplication is seen in the ministry of a friend of mine in India. All he needs to begin a church is a good shade tree, and a church is born, not just in one place, but wherever he can find a tree and collect enough people.

*The Status Quo, Divided by Chaos, Multiplied by Risk Taking, Equals Opportunities for Change*

The established church that turns into the storm will find chaos is always a precursor to the radical change of an established system. Those leaders who want change create just enough chaos to destabilize the system. Any transition requires that the status quo becomes destabilized long and hard enough to catch the controllers off guard. This allows leaders to take major risks and instigate a major change. So the established church that thrives mid-storm will be in continuous chaos until emerging on the other side of the storm, only to find another storm waiting.

In the emerging world, new forms of life always self-organize out of the chaos, if the chaos is sustained long enough.

So the established church in the future will not be as predictable as it was during modernity, nor will it be as peaceful. In whatever form the church takes, the thriving church will be led by risk takers who, like the captain of a ship, turn into the storm and embrace chaos without fear to find the sun shining on the other side of the storm.

As we move from modernity to whatever is to come, most established churches will face enormous periods of discontinuity and chaos. Those who take advantage of the storm and make radical changes will carve out a niche for themselves. Those who do not have no chance of survival.

*Opportunities for Change, Multiplied by Continuous Chaos, Equals New Bursts of Ministry and Motivation*

When a dead system is burst open and kept open, people with hope in their hearts seize the moment and self-organize for ministry, creating new opportunities for change. That's the way organic systems function. In such a situation, leaders must be flexible and quick to respond to opportunities.

Organic systems never follow predictable paths or grow the same way, so don't be *surprised* when you're surprised. Dreamers are never surprised—just delighted. Leaders have to believe in the possibilities of what might happen when people are set free. So dream big and avoid the recurring nightmares.

*Opportunities for Change, Multiplied by Continuous Chaos, Minus Leadership, Equals Disaster*

The future church will require a stronger, more focused, single leader than ever before. A ship can have only one captain when it turns into a storm. Anything else is disaster.

I know a lot has been written about team-based ministry, and I'm all for it, as long as the team has a single leader. Every thriving form of life has one, single, organizing principle. The same is true for the church. The church will need leaders who lead and who do not blink in times of chaos.

Three forms of church governance dominate the church landscape today: congregational, representative democracy, and apostolic, or pastor-led. Due to the perfect storm, only one will dominate the twenty-first century. Feelings usually run high as to which one of these is the best form of governance. However, most of the churches using forms of congregational or representative democracy are leftovers from modernity and are on life support. On the other hand, the vast majority of thriving churches today are apostolic, or pastor-led. We've also noted that the thriving churches using congregational and representative forms of governance have figured out how to circumvent as much of their governance systems as possible.

Over the past twenty years, I have had the opportunity to observe some of America's most authentic and effective pastors. One quality stands out above all the rest in every one of these pastors—they pastor as spiritual leaders who listen to God rather than as corporate leaders who lead based on democratic rule.

Even if these pastors function in a denomination that requires democratic rule, they find ways to get around or minimize its effects and provide biblical leadership.

Thus, a rule of thumb in the twenty-first century is, the less democracy in the church the more authentic and effective the church is in advancing the kingdom of God! To some, this sounds like heresy. But when you think about it, voting and democracy are not found in the scriptures. So why are they part of so many churches today? We have acquiesced to culture rather than followed the scriptures. The thriving church in the twenty-first century will change that mistake.

*Leadership, Minus Controllers and Meetings, Plus an Ample Supply of Apprentices, Multiplied by Equipping Ministries, Equals an Army of Trained Recruits*

The thriving future church will focus on the penetration of the people of God into the world rather than the maintenance of the institution. Authentic congregations are always moving away from themselves into the world. The more equipped people the church is sending out into the world to change it, the more the church is functioning like a New Testament church.

One of the primary responsibilities of leaders is to mentor and equip apprentices to follow Jesus on the road to mission. Leaders know that when they release people to do whatever ministry God has called and gifted them to do, the Kingdom experiences the joy of exponential people growth. It is far more beneficial to the Kingdom to have people serving in the world than sitting in another meeting at the church. So they tell their people—if you are spending more than two hours at church a week, it is too much. Any ideas here?

*An Army of Recruits, Plus Involvement in Ministry, Plus Minimal Cognitive Learning, Multiplied by On-The-Job Training, Minus Professional Clergy, Equals a Trained Army of Mobilized Servants*

Most of the pastors and staff of the church of the future will bypass formal religious education and go straight into working in or planting a church. Like Jesus, they will be self-trained and focus on results rather than education. As a result, emphasis in leadership will shift from religious leader to spiritual guide. Laity will not expect the pastor to do ministry on their behalf but to be the one who guides them into ministry. Leaders in thriving churches today are already witnesses to this mid-storm equation.

We have learned on a mission field the quicker a seeker is involved in ministry to others, the more likely that person is to experience salvation and become a servant.

People are always asking me what curriculum they should use to equip people for ministry. I love the expression on their faces when I tell them, "You are the curriculum. Just let them hang out with you."

The twenty-first-century church is learning the lost art of having apprentices learn a trade by actually practicing that trade. In our case, the trade is following Jesus. Following Jesus requires far more than learning the Bible or taking a course at church. Sure, every leader needs some cognitive learning. But we do not need to be cognitive captives. Learning to be a leader requires hanging out on the mission field, getting one's hands and heart dirty for Jesus. And guess what? Hanging out doesn't cost anything!

*Mobilized Servants, Plus a Supportive Structure and Organization, Multiplied by Prayer, Minus Planning, Equals Pure Energy*

Something that is often overlooked in the process of mobilizing a congregation is the need for a prayer-filled structure and organization. The mechanical, institutionally based established church of modernity has little understanding of the power of prayer. Instead, during modernity the established church learned to function around planning. A strategic plan would save the day; not so in the future. The ministry of the thriving church today arises out of prayer more than planning. When it all boils down to the bottom line, prayer is the "maker or breaker" in how well the army of God moves through a community, changing lives and breaking down barriers to humanity.

*Effective Pure Energy, Equals the Mass of the Congregation, Squared by How Fast It Can Change*

$E=mc^2$ is one of the most famous equations known to humanity. It basically says that energy equals mass multiplied by the square of the speed of light. In the same way, the future belongs only to those who can change the fastest and with the least amount of angst. One of the things this definitely rules out is fixating on anything that is *annual*—like annual budgets or annual meetings. The emerging world moves far too fast for anything based on a year. Instead, the future church flies by the seat of its pants, not merely responding to life, but creating the circumstances in which it does ministry. The future church understands it is the weakest yet most powerful force in the universe and acts accordingly. Nothing is impossible to those in whom Christ dwells.

### *Balance, Plus Status Quo, Equals Decline and Eventually Death*

Balance usually means to do nothing and keep everything equal. Do nothing and your church is sure to die.

In a recent book, *Unfreezing Moves*, I challenged the classic view of change that instructs the change agent to unfreeze the system, make a change, and then refreeze the system to allow the new change to gain a foothold. This is a formula for disaster in a world defined by speed. Instead, the future church will keep the system alive, unfrozen, and chaotic. Like an organism, the church is allowed to expand any way it can. For this to happen, leaders have to be flexible and open to the spontaneous movement of the Spirit. The last thing they seek is balance.

This equation has enormous implications for congregational life. It reveals the foolishness of anything set in concrete other than the DNA of the congregation—mission, vision, values, and bedrock beliefs. Consider all of the things congregations set in concrete for a year or even longer: budgets, programs, salaries—even the Christian calendar. Such a mind-set is foreign to the emerging new world. Why not start thinking about budgets in daily, monthly, or quarterly form instead of yearly? Better yet, stop thinking budgets and start thinking about liquid pools of money from which any one of the core ministries can draw.

Now you can see why it is so imperative that congregations get clear about their core mission and the values and beliefs that will sustain such a mission. You can see why it is so critical to have leaders who tenaciously guard this mission as well as remove all the barriers to its realization. Leaders, like the shepherds of old, see it as their primary responsibility to provide safe pastures in which their flock can graze and thus grow in their relationship to God, themselves, and others. The primary role of leadership today is to guide people on their journey into the emerging world and, when it is necessary, to turn the ship headlong into the storm.

## Heading into the Storm

I'm sure you can come up with more equations we should be learning. So add to the list by e-mailing me at Easum@aol.com.

Now set sail into the emerging world and watch out for the storms. Oops. Look on the horizon!

CHAPTER NINE

# The Tides Are Turning

MICHAEL BLEWETT *(United States)*

*The great storm is coming, but the tide has turned.*

SAINT GANDALF THE WHITE[1]

## An Unexpected Gift—The Tide Turns

I turned forty years old on Sunday, April 2, 2006. That morning, while administering Communion at our 9:15 service, I received an unexpected birthday gift, a tide-turning[2] moment. If you've ever received Communion before, you might have wondered what is going through the mind of the priest as he is placing the consecrated bread in your hands. Sometimes our thoughts are very pious, but our minds do wander just like anyone else's. During a changeover at the altar rail—when a new row of folks come forward to receive—I was thinking about the birthday party I would be throwing myself later that evening. And then the gift arrived: "You've spent your first forty years trying to be right; now it's time to be in right relationship."

It was one of those unmistakable moments when I knew God was speaking. The gift was permission to rely on relationship, on connection. It was an invitation to wholeness, to *shalom*, to perfection.[3] Relationship is the rich, fertile humus in which we grow into the glory of God, where we become fully human, fully alive.[4]

## I Love Jim Cantore

Jim Cantore is one of my heroes. You may not know who Jim is and probably couldn't pick him out while waiting for your latte at Starbucks. But if I dressed Jim in waterproof gear, lashed him to a palm tree, and stuck a microphone in his hand, your amnesia would vanish. Truth be told, you don't want Jim Cantore showing up at your local Starbucks, because if Jim's in town, your town is in trouble. While everyone else catches the nearest plane, train, automobile, or moped to get out of Dodge, Jim sets sail in his dinghy and rows into the belly of the beast. "Jim's passion for field reporting during extreme weather events is well-known among TWC viewers. Whether it's 'thunder snow,' an ice storm, tornado chasing or a Category 5 hurricane, there is no place Jim would rather be than right in the 'eye of the storm.'"[5]

Jim's level of intimacy with weather events is something thrilling, immersive, and transformative. It is dangerous for him and potentially lifesaving for us. Would anyone you know talk about the church's relationship with popular culture the same way: dangerous for us and life-saving for others?

## In and Around: You Are Not a Weather Pattern

You may not be a weather nerd like me, but do you watch weather forecasts? Growing up on the shores of Lake Huron, I learned to pay attention to forecasts. If you listen to weather people, they use an interesting little phrase, *in and around*. "There's a 90 percent chance of showers in-and-around Saint Louis this afternoon," or "There were massive power outages in and around the bi-state area as a result of the ice storm." *In and around* is a handy phrase for forecasters; it offers specificity and generality at the same time, a way of hedging your bets when predicting the effects of something as large and mysterious as a weather system. *In and around* is good for forecasters; it's deadly for fore*tasters* of the Kingdom.

You are not a weather system. You cannot be in *and* around anything. You are a punctilious person; you can be in or around, not in *and* around. It's like trying to be only a little bit pregnant. You can't do it; you are, or you aren't. You are either in relationship, or you are around a relationship.

During Jesus' ministry, there were concentric circles around him. Peter, James, and John appear to have been the closest, those in the innermost circle. Moving outward, we see the rest of the Twelve, then those who followed Jesus around, then the curious crowds, and, finally, the outright enemies of Jesus. Out of all these, I think the most dangerous place to be is in the midst of the crowd. I know the danger of making gross generalizations, but it's the crowd—those who are just *around* Jesus, never *in* or *with* Jesus—that end up moving Jesus from celebration to condemnation to crucifixion. In a narrative heartbeat, the crowd moves from holy huzzahs to hate-filled harangues. Their affections change like, well, the weather. Their hosannas are accompanied by the waving of palms; their condemnation ("Crucify him!"[6]) with waving fists of fury. And the result of only dabbling in discipleship is not rebuke from Jesus, but *self*-condemnation: "His blood be on us and on our children."[7]

The call of Jesus is unambiguous. I can imagine Jesus saying, "You're either with me or against me, but don't ever be 'kinda-sorta.'" God would much rather deal with your ecstasy or enmity; God can't do *anything* with apathy. The ancient reflection of this love/hate relationship between God and God's people can be found in Psalms. You don't have to spend much time in them to discover that they aren't all sweetness, light, and strawberries-and-cream latte. It doesn't take long for the singers (psalms are supposed to be sung, are they not?) to go from raving to raging. The curious thing is that God wants both. I'm actually glad that there's a movement within atheism today that is much more aggressive than in the past.[8] God can do something with aggression, nothing with agnosticism. This point was made very clear to me in a neonatal intensive care unit.

During seminary, I did some training at Saint Luke's Episcopal Hospital in Houston. We chaplains-in-training were sent out, two-by-two, to respond to the many and varied pastoral calls that surfaced. One afternoon, I was paired with a well-meaning Unitarian woman who was trying to comfort a woman in the throes of having just lost her child. Trying to defend her concept of God, she said to the grieving mother, "I know you're angry right now, but God had nothing to do with the death of your baby." I saw the mother's face redden as she rounded on my partner *du jour*. "Don't you tell me that! If God's not involved in this, then there's *no hope at all!*"

## Anatomy of a Storm

It starts with a stirring. Maybe it's the proverbial butterfly flapping its wings at a distance, or maybe it's the movement of the once-hovering Spirit; the storm starts with a stirring. The strongest of storms, a hurricane, needs three basic things to form and become formidable: wind, water, and warmth.

When I lived in Houston for a short time, I used to quip that, being a "storm aficionado," I'd like to experience a hurricane. Longtime residents, who had lived through Camille (August 17, 1969), quickly let me know what an idiotic wish that was. Now, it seems, I'm living in the midst of a Spirit-storm the likes of which the church has not seen. Before I recognized the waves for what they were, I was tempted to post-Camille (post-Katrina?) despair. Now I am more convinced than ever that the swells we see are not caused by the thrashing of Leviathan.[9] They are the sign of the One who "tramples the waves of the Sea."[10]

God is busy. The Spirit is blowing wherever it will; the annoying thing for the Church is that the Spirit isn't always where we will. If God can speak through the mouth of Balaam's donkey,[11] why are we shocked that God might use some of the jackasses from popular culture? The Spirit still enlivens and strengthens and moves the church, but when churches won't budge—like stubborn asses—the Spirit has no choice but to make waves in places we can't see because we haven't bothered to go.

I think we may have become addicted to an analogy. Remember Elijah on Mount Horeb?[12] The Lord was not in the wind, earthquake, or fire; Elijah heard God in a "still small voice"[13] The church has been engaged in collective "navel-gazing" for some time now, expecting a repeat of the still, small voice. However, between 1 Kings and right now, God has spoken in a new way, in an ancient Word. His voice is "as the sound of rushing waters."[14] In order to really hear that voice, you and I have to head out where the waters are *ruah*-roiled.

## Back to You, Jim

When Jim Cantore is on location in the midst of a hurricane, you can always count on one thing: the report from the eye of the storm. In the midst of an eerie calm, Jim and his camera crew pan around to give those of us on the sidelines some sense of the devastation. Although I'm sure the eye of a hurricane is a cool thing to experience, I'm equally sure that it cannot remotely compare to the thrill of being tossed in the tempest. The eye of the storm is a great place for reporting but a lousy place to surf.

Many of our churches have become like eyes in the midst of this perfect storm. We preachers report on the cultural devastation being wreaked outside our walls, all the while bemoaning the fact that the air inside is anything but Spirit-stirred. The air inside has become still; if it's not dead, it's certainly on life-support. It's time to open the windows and put it on *love*-support.

## Water-indissoluble, Spirit-stirred Relationships

When I was a boy, I remember complaining to my mother because we were caught between the store and the parked car without an umbrella in a rainstorm. In her wonderful way, she just said, "Come on, you won't melt." Since then I've been caught without an umbrella many times, and I have even been known to walk out in a powerful storm on purpose. It's not a bad thing to get drenched to the bone.

In the introduction to the baptismal rite from the *Book of Common Prayer*, you'll find the following statement:

> Holy Baptism is full initiation by water and the Holy Spirit into Christ's Body the Church. The bond which God establishes in Baptism is indissoluble.[15]

If the storm we are in the midst of is of God—and I do believe that is the case—then I am sure of at least two things: we will get soaked, and we will become stronger.

When I speak of getting soaked, I am talking about relationship. Relationship is a *given* for the baptized; we cannot avoid it. We are intimately and *indissolubly* connected to Jesus and those whom Jesus loves. And because Jesus loves some pretty difficult people, our lives will be messy and merciful and, therefore, memorable.

Getting waterworn also makes us stronger. Water is insidious and unstoppable. It can go anywhere, find the lowest point, and seep into every cranny. Unfortunately, my church doesn't have an immersion pool, so I pour water over the heads of the candidates. I always remind folks that, even though they aren't getting completely wet, the water is getting hold of all of them.

Water is the great solvent, isn't it? But baptismal water is much more like Krazy Glue. The Body of Christ, the body of the baptized, is a body comprised of broken bones.[16] Baptism, by the power of water and the Spirit, knits those broken bones together, making them stronger than they were before the break occurred.

Once we've been thoroughly soaked, the Spirit-stirred wind whips around us, over us, and through us. The wind dries us and cures us. Anyone who has ever been dried by the wind after a dip in the ocean knows what is left: a fine layer of salt. You are the salt of the earth.[17] Many in the church, I fear, have come dangerously close to losing their saltiness because of a question that goes unasked.

## The Most Unasked Question

I've been involved in Christian ministry almost my entire life, in just about every facet of lay and ordained ministry. I've led many people, from adolescents to adults, to a knowledge and love of the Lord. I've celebrated Eucharist, baptized babies, blessed marriages, comforted the dying, and buried the dead. I've climbed mountains, rappelled off cliffs and floated down rivers for the sake of God's kingdom. In the midst of all these tribulations and triumphs, I've been asked so many different spiritual and theological questions that I've lost count.

A couple years ago, while driving home after celebrating an evening Eucharist, I was accosted by another question. I had just finished preaching a "homilette"[18] in which I referenced the most asked question of clergy, namely, "How do I know when God is speaking to me?" But on my short drive home, another question came to me: "What is the most unasked question?" And as surprising as the question was, more surprising was the immediacy with which I knew the answer: "Is this all there is?"

That question is un*asked* because it's un*settling*. An apparent chasm has been fixed, separating the great story of salvation and our perception of everyday experience. We are gathered[19] from our dwellings on Sundays to hear accounts like Peter's first sermon,[20] after which three thousand people came to believe. We marvel at how the ill could be healed simply by placing them in the path of Peter's shadow.[21] Most haunting to me are phrases like 1 Peter 1:8:

> Although you have not seen him, you love him; and even though you do not see him now, you believe in him and rejoice with an indescribable and glorious joy.

Indescribable and glorious joy. How many folks have you met whose lives you would describe with that phrase? Does one look back at you in the mirror each morning?

Chances are, you answered that question in the negative; most people answer that way, most of the time. But I've come to believe (although I realize it far too infrequently) that this kind of joy—indescribable and glorious joy—is doable, attainable, and sustainable.

The joy is not in the journey; it's in the relationships. The joy isn't found where the rubber meets the road, but where I meet you, in Christ. It's not about me becoming we; it's about us becoming him.

Some are fond of saying, "It's not the destination; it's the journey."

Some folks flip that into, "It's not the journey; it's the destination."

Other variations I've heard include "It's not the journey or the destination, but what you do when you arrive," and "It's not about journeys or destinations, but how you look while you travel."

Since my tide-turning birthday gift, I now say, "It's not *just* about the journey or the destination; it's about those with whom you travel."

There's a wonderful double meaning in that. For eons, Christians have been imagining what questions we might be asked when we meet God face-to-face. My favorite is, "Where are the others?"

Who are you bringing with you into the Kingdom? If you can answer that question, you know something about indescribable and glorious joy.

The other meaning points directly to the One who is our "companion on the Way."[22] Our journey this side of eternity is about becoming Christ,[23] living and loving his life into the world. He is the journey, he is the destination, and he is the one with whom we travel. He is the Calmer of the storm, and, more importantly, the One who calms us in the storm.

Did you ever notice that, after you've been on the road for a while, you begin resembling your traveling companions? Don't believe me? Then you probably don't have kids. Anyone who has ever endured screaming children in the back seat will understand what I am saying. How long does it take before road rage hits? And remember that road trip you took with your college cronies? Did you do anything you might not normally have done because there was safety, or stupidity, in numbers? Perfect stormers, Jesus' storm troopers, engage in activities that others might deem stupid or unsafe.

## Safety

The Archbishop of Canterbury, Rowan Williams, recently published a statement: "Church must be 'safe place' for gay and lesbian people."[24] The human sexuality debate is part of a particularly violent band of thunderstorms pummeling my tribe (the Episcopal Church) at the moment. Now, let me be very clear: I deplore any act of violence committed because of sexual orientation or behavior. I understand that there are parts of the world, including here in the "enlightened West," where persecution occurs due to race, creed, color, gender, sexual preference, and a host of other reasons.

I am also concerned about what we mean by *safety* or being a *safe place* where the church is concerned. I'm not aware of any place in the gospel where Jesus promises us safety or security. He does promise a cross.

I am suspicious that when people hear the word *safety* they automatically interpret it as safety *from*. Safety *from* violence and persecution can easily devolve into safety *from* conviction and repentance. If I say that the church is a safe place with respect to rich people or alcoholics or adulterers, I could be taken to mean that Jesus loves you as you are and doesn't expect transformation. Yes, Jesus loves us, not primarily for who we are, but as *he knows us to be*.

If there is any safety in the church (and that is a big *if*), it is a safety *for*. Safety *for* doing radically connective things like loving your neighbor as yourself, loving your enemy as your neighbor, and loving yourself not as you are, but as God knows you to be in Christ. To quote Mr. Beaver from *The Lion, the Witch and the Wardrobe:*

> Who said anything about safe? 'Course he isn't safe. But he's good. He's the King, I tell you.[25]

## Radical Connection

I heard a sermon recently in which the preacher spoke in praise of radical inclusion. I've been around long enough to know what the phrase *radical inclusion* means these days. It almost always alludes to a kind of self-esteem-building, I'm-OK-you're-OK kind of approach that makes me very uneasy.

This is the usual approach: "Jesus is all about love and tolerance" or "Jesus ate with prostitutes and tax collectors" or "Who am I to judge?" It reminds me of a formation class I was teaching last year when a well-meaning person in the class stated, "I love this church because it's a come-as-you-are church!" I said, "Yes it is, but it's not a stay-as-you-are church." Life-in-Christ is a transforming endeavor. In fact, it might be even more than that; it might be as shocking and jarring as the sudden shift from darkness to light. As Paul says in 2 Corinthians, "If anyone is in Christ; new creation!"[26]

Even though Jesus did "eat good food with bad people,"[27] those same people also had the unignorable tendency to change their manner of life. They experienced a freedom of life in perfect service to the Lord of life. It was not freedom as license to do what they wanted; their wants were transformed by their relationship with Jesus.

The gospel is not, as popularly stated, about radical inclusion, but about radical connection. It is that connection that prompts God, who "so loved the world that he gave his only Son."[28] It is that connection that leads the Son to die for us "while we were still sinners."[29]

Radical inclusion is about being all you can be now that you've gotten rid of your guilt. Radical connection is about being Christ and living his life into the world.

## Stretching and Striking

Stormy church fights always elicit creative vocabulary from the opposing camps. One of the favorite phrases used by Episcopalians who are *dialoging* (we are far too nice to actually *fight*) is *living in tension*. I'd be okay with that if that was actually what was taking place. But it's not. We are not in tension; we are in conflict.

The root of the word *tension* is from the Latin *tensionem*, which means "a stretching." *Conflict*, on the other hand, is from *conflictus*, "to strike together." Lately, I've seen far more striking than stretching. Don't get me wrong: I do think that we need a good knock-down, drag-out fight in the church from time to time. I imagine that the Council of Nicaea had far more in common with Wrestlemania than *Robert's Rules of Order*. I'm also not advocating a big, fat group hug where we all pretend that everything is okay.

The stretching I'm proposing is a reaching out toward the lost, toward those who are not yet in relationship with their Savior. Jesus is the model for our stretching and striking: he "stretched out [his] arms of love on the hard wood of the cross that everyone might come within the reach of His saving embrace."[30] And we struck him for it.

Are we willing to be soaked, salted, and struck for Jesus' sake and the sake of the world he loves? God has birthed you into this particular storm at this particular time for a particular purpose. We can huddle in the basement, hoping and praying that the storm will blow over, or we can go outside and play in the Godly gale.

# CHAPTER TEN

# The Relationships of Winds and Waves

MARK BATTERSON *(United States)*

*The cross must be raised again at the center of the marketplace as well as on the steeple of the church. I am claiming that Jesus was not crucified in a cathedral between two candles, but on a cross between two thieves; on the town garbage heap, at a crossroads so cosmopolitan they had to write His title in Hebrew, Latin, and Greek. At the kind of place where cynics talk smut, and thieves curse, and soldiers gamble, because that is where He died and that is what he died about and that is where churchmen ought to be and what churchmen should be about.*

GEORGE MCLEOD[1]

A few years ago I had a Starbucks moment. I was studying for a sermon at a Starbucks on Capitol Hill. I usually tune out the mood music, but one line of lyrics slipped through my reticular activating system. I'd never heard the song before and I didn't know who the artist was. And maybe I just had too much caffeine in my system, but the juxtaposition of the words I heard struck me: the song described a church on the periphery by the name of Lady of our Epiphany.

And I had a thought as I sipped my vanilla latte: as long as the church stays on the periphery, our culture will never experience an epiphany.

Over the last few decades, the church has been pushed further and further onto the periphery of culture. Or in many instances, the church has retreated to the comfortable confines of its Christian subculture. So we are inside our churches looking out, but we really find ourselves on the outside looking in. God is calling the church out of the church and back into the middle of the marketplace.

I realize that I pastor one church in one small corner of the Kingdom. And I don't want to project my passions onto others. But if we are going to turn the spiritual tide in America, the church needs to stop retreating and start redeeming. The church needs to stop criticizing and start creating. The church needs to stop seeking shelter and start chasing the storm.

Paul didn't boycott the Aeropagus.[2] He didn't stand outside in a picket line arguing against idolatry. Paul marched into the marketplace of ideas and went toe-to-toe with the most brilliant minds in ancient Athens competing for the truth. Staying on the periphery is one thing the apostle Paul could never be accused of. And although some Bible scholars question the success of his ministry in Athens, don't tell that to Dionysius or Damaris! And here is my concern: if the church boycotts the Aeropagus, we'll lose the Dionysiuses and Damarises of our generation!

## Church Steeples

There was a time, just a few centuries ago, when nautical maps of Europe had legends that included the location of churches on land, and church steeples doubled as navigational tools for ship captains. Nothing was more visible on the premodern skyline than church steeples.

Churches were typically built on choice real estate in the center of town or atop the highest hill, and, in some places, there were ordinances against building anything taller than the church steeple so it would occupy the place closest to heaven.[3] In a sense, church steeples symbolized the place of the church in culture. The church was the center of culture. Church was the place to go. Church was the thing to do. Nothing was more visible than the church steeple. Nothing was more audible than the church bells. And it might be a slight exaggeration, but all the premodern church had to do was raise a steeple and ring a bell.

Is it safe to say that things have changed?

The church no longer enjoys a cultural monopoly. We are the minority in post-Christian America. And the significance of that is this: we can't afford to do church the way it's always been done. Our tactics must change.

Don't get me wrong: the message is sacred. But methods are not. The moment we make our methods sacrosanct, we stop creating the future and start repeating the past. We stop doing ministry out of imagination and start doing ministry out of memory. If we think that raising the steeple or ringing the bells will get the job done, the church in America will end up right where the Israelites found themselves in Judges 2:10 NLT:

> After that generation died, another generation grew up who did not acknowledge the LORD or remember the mighty things he had done for Israel.

According to George Barna, 61 percent of twenty-somethings who grew up going to church *stop* going to church at some point during their twenties. They become *dechurched*. They still feel connected to God in some form or fashion, but there is a disconnect with organized religion and the institutional church. And for one reason or another, they are checking out of the church at an alarming rate.

I love the church. I believe in the church. I've poured ten years of blood, sweat, and tears into the church that I have the privilege of pastoring—National Community Church in Washington DC. But the church needs to change! And change always starts with some honest self-reflection.

Some people hear statistics like the one just cited—61 percent of twenty-somethings that grew up in church leave the church—and they wonder what's wrong with *this generation*. That is the wrong reaction. I can't help wondering what's wrong with *the church*.

In the words of Pogo: *we have seen the enemy and he is us.*

You may not want to read what I'm about to write, and I don't want to write what you're about to read, but the post-Christian church needs to repent of irrelevance.

God isn't just omnipotent, omnipresent, and omniscient. God is omnirelevant. God knows every thought that fires across your synapses. God orders every footstep. God knows the number of hairs on your head. And God is fluent in billions of individual dialects. God is absolutely and infinitely relevant. But I'm afraid that, all too often, we cast a suspicious glance at relevant churches and falsely assume that they must be dumbing down or watering down the gospel. Maybe we've got it backwards? Maybe relevant churches are taking the incarnation seriously? Sure, all of us have seen examples of churches that turn the gospel into a gimmick. It's inexcusable! But that doesn't excuse irrelevance. If we are truly following in the footsteps of Jesus, we must walk the tightrope between biblical authenticity and cultural relevancy.

Permission to speak frankly? Too many pastors are getting A's in biblical exegesis and D's in cultural exegesis. We know Scripture, but we're out of touch with the times. The end result is a gap between theology and reality called irrelevance. We're out of touch with the very people we're trying to reach—the unchurched and dechurched. We've got to exegete our culture so we can close the gap. That's what incarnation is all about.

The post-Christian church needs a revelation: *irrelevance is irreverence!*

## Now Meeting at a Theater near You

I entered the church-planting arena ten years ago with the traditional mind-set: meet in rented facilities until you can buy or build a church building. And then our church started meeting in the movie theaters at Union Station, four blocks from the Capitol. More than twenty-five million people pass through the station every year, making it the most visited destination in the nation's capital. We have forty food court restaurants right outside our front entrance. We have large movie screens and comfortable theater seats. And not only do we have a bus stop, train stop, and parking garage. We have our own subway system that drops off right at our front door.

Every once in a while, someone will ask me when we're going to get a church. The question is innocent enough and I'm sure it's well-intentioned, but it does belie a common misconception. Let me clear it up: *the church is not a building*. You can't *go* to church because you are the church! Besides, why build a church when you've got a Union Station?

It's hard to imagine a more strategic spiritual beachhead than Union Station, and somewhere along the way I had a paradigm shift. Actually, I remember exactly where I was. I was walking home from Union Station, and I had a vision at the corner of 5th and F streets, NE. There weren't any angelic choirs. No graffiti on the wall. But it was definitely a road-to-Damascus experience (Acts 9:3). We were still a neophyte church trying to get one location established, but I could envision multiple NCC locations dotting the metro map. I felt like God was calling us to meet in movie theaters at metro stops throughout the Washington DC area.

Over the past decade, National Community Church has morphed into one church with multiple locations. And along with our movie theater locations, we own and operate Ebenezers, the largest coffeehouse on Capitol Hill. It was also voted the number two coffeehouse in the DC metro area by *AOL CityGuide* in 2007. Ebenezers is a place where the church and community cross paths seven days a week and the performance space doubles as our Saturday night studio, where we have two services that are recorded in high-definition for replay at our movie theater locations.

The driving motivation behind building a coffeehouse instead of a church building was a pretty simple observation from the Gospels. Jesus didn't hang out at synagogues. Jesus hung out at wells. Wells were more than just a place to draw water. Wells were *natural gathering places* in ancient culture. Jesus didn't expect people to come to him. He crossed ancient cultural boundaries and went to them. And that is what the incarnation is all about.

So instead of building a traditional church building where people gather once a week, we built a postmodern well where people gather all day, every day. And instead of water, we serve coffee—coffee with a cause.

One interesting footnote: According to coffee lore, the church may be responsible for the popularity of coffee. Way back in the sixteenth century, advisors to Pope Clement VIII wanted him to declare coffee a drink of the devil because of its popularity amongst Muslims. Pope Clement must have liked his double shot of espresso because it's reported that he said, "this devil's drink is so good . . . we should cheat the devil by baptizing it."

Ebenezers serves baptized coffee!

## Church and Culture

As I see it, the church has four options when it comes to engaging culture: ignore it, imitate it, condemn it, or create it. And each option leads in very different directions.

We can *ignore* culture, but the by-product of ignorance is irrelevance. The more we ignore culture the more irrelevant we'll become. And *if the church ignores the culture, the culture will ignore the church.*

We can *imitate* culture, but imitation is a form of suicide. Originality is sacrificed on the altar of cultural conformity. *If we don't shape the culture, the culture will shape us.*

We can *condemn* culture, but condemnation is a cop out. Let me just call it what it is: condemnation is spiritual laziness. We've got to stop pointing the finger and start offering better alternatives. *If the church condemns the culture, the culture will condemn the church.*

Those three options will lead the church down a dead-end road to irrelevance, but there is another option—the only option if we're serious about fulfilling the Great Commission and incarnating the gospel. We can engage culture by *creating culture.*

In the immortal words of the Italian artist and poet Michelangelo: *criticize by creating.*

At the end of the day, the culture will treat the church the way the church treats the culture. And we're not called to condemn. We're called to redeem.

## Cultural Capital

As spiritual leaders, we have to do more than exegete Scripture. We have to exegete the culture. So let me confront the issue: it is difficult to *demand attention* if we don't *pay attention*. If we talk without listening, what we have to say is viewed as a diatribe. And we'll keep answering questions no one is asking!

A few years ago someone paid me a compliment that caught me off guard. They thanked me for quoting nonbiblical sources in my messages. No one had ever commented on that component of my communication, but that compliment has become part of my philosophy of preaching. I love to read, and I'm interested in just about everything, so it's not uncommon for me to quote anyone from Aristotle and Heraclitus to Gladwell and Goleman. And what I realized is this. Quoting Scripture gives me credibility with Christians. Quoting nonbiblical sources gives me credibility with non-Christians. And whereas our nonbiblical sources should never be unbiblical, we have to recognize that cross-pollinating with nontheological disciplines gives us cultural capital.

Every year we do two series titled *God @ the Box Office* and *God @ the Billboards* that explore spiritual themes in popular movies and songs. The reason is simple: the 60 percent of Americans who don't attend church get their theology from movies and music. For better or for worse, moviemakers and musicians are the chief theologians in our culture.

In the prophetic words of the eighteenth-century Scottish thinker Andrew Fletcher: "if a man were permitted to make all the ballads he need not care who should make the laws of a nation."[4]

Our culture is shaped, even more than we realize, by the movies we watch and the music we listen to. And we have a choice. We can ignore them. We can condemn them. Or we can dialogue about them. *God @ the Box Office* and *God @ the Billboards* are attempts to exegete the movies and music that shape the cultural consciousness of nearly two hundred million unchurched Americans. We exegete the scripts and lyrics and juxtapose them with Scripture. And although a series on movies or music may sound like watered-down or dumbed-down versions of the gospel, they are actually two of our hardest-hitting sermon series because movies and music are brutally honest about the human condition. And in a sense, movies and songs are idols to an unknown god. We need to use them as spiritual leverage much like Paul used the idol to an unknown god in Athens.

We need to get serious about exegeting culture and finding spiritual identification points. We need to redeem cultural metaphors to communicate the gospel. Isn't that what Jesus did as a parabolist? He framed truth in ways that fit within the cognitive categories of his listeners.

If we choose to ignore the culture around us, we aren't following in the footsteps of Jesus. We're only digging our own grave and burying ourselves alive.

## Sanctified Competitive Streak

When I first started pastoring, I really struggled with keeping my competitive streak in check. I found myself comparing myself to other pastors as pastors are prone to do. But that only leads down one of two paths: pride or jealousy. I knew it was unhealthy and unholy to make those comparisons. So I asked God to crucify my competitive streak, but no matter how many times I asked, it kept resurrecting. And then I had a revelation. I realized that God didn't want to kill my competitive streak. God wanted to intensify it. God wanted to redirect it. God wanted to sanctify it and use it for God's purposes!

There is no place for competition within the Kingdom. But God wants to channel our competitive streak in healthy and holy directions. We are called to be incarnationists.

In his book, *Roaring Lambs*, Bob Briner reflects on missionary conventions he went to as a child where people were challenged to commit themselves to missions. And thank God for missionaries and missionary conventions! But Briner suggests that maybe we need to expand our definition of a missionary to include Christians who are called into culture-shaping professions like journalism, entertainment, education, business, and politics. Bob Briner says, "I envision a whole generation of roaring lambs who will lay claim to these careers with the same vigor and commitment that sent men like Hudson Taylor to China."[5]

I think the church has allowed a false dichotomy between *secular* and *sacred* to creep into our worldview. We have divided occupations into spiritual and nonspiritual when, the truth is, every Christian ought to pursue his or her career as a God-ordained calling. Doctors ought to feel just as called to medicine as pastors feel called to ministry, so should teachers and politicians and artists. The church needs to commission writers and actors and entrepreneurs and politicians just as we do pastors!

We are called to be culture-shapers. In the words of Bob Briner,

> Why not believe that one day the most critically acclaimed director in Hollywood could be an active Christian layman in his church? Why not hope that the Pulitzer Prize for investigative reporting could go to a Christian journalist on staff at a major daily newspaper? Is it really too much of a stretch to think that a major exhibit at the Museum of Modern Art could feature the works of an artist on staff at one of our Christian colleges? Am I out of my mind to suggest that your son or daughter could be the principal dancer for the Joffrey Ballet Company, leading a weekly Bible study for other dancers in what was once considered a profession that was morally bankrupt?[6]

## Facing the Giants

A few months ago, I came across a brilliant example of cultural exegesis. An ordained pastor turned movie director, Alex Kendrick, decided to incarnate the gospel by producing a movie. *Facing the Giants* caught the attention of the mainstream media because the cast and crew were members of Sherwood Baptist Church in Albany, Georgia.

I met Alex Kendrick right after the movie released. He happened to be having coffee at our coffeehouse on Capitol Hill in between congressional meetings. And he told me the story behind the movie. The genesis of the movie was a study on cultural influencers. It didn't come as a great surprise to Kendrick that movies and television topped the list. But he was dismayed at the fact that the church was nowhere to be found. It didn't even crack the top-ten list of cultural influencers. So Kendrick and Sherwood Baptist Church made a decision: if people aren't going to come to church, then maybe the church needs to go the movies. They turned their congregation into cast and crew. Some members acted in the film. Others made meals or watched children or built movie sets. The church rallied around the vision. And instead of criticizing immorality in entertainment, they created an entertainment alternative with an incarnational message. My meeting with Alex took place right after the movie released, and there had already been 471 decisions for Christ. What a redefinition of what it means to be a missional church!

And it is an example of what happens when a church decides to compete for the Kingdom. It is an example of what happens when a church takes the Great Commission seriously. It is an example of what happens when a church finds a creative way to incarnate the gospel message.

I have a core conviction that drives me: *there are ways of doing church that no one has thought of yet.*

I honestly believe that our best days are in front of us. Our generation has an unprecedented opportunity to fulfill the Great Commission if we simply redeem the technology at our disposal and use it for God's purposes.

The church must not run away or shrink back from the cultural storm. We're called to storm the gates of hell.

*Carpe* culture!

CHAPTER ELEVEN

# Between Spirit and Culture

THOMAS G. BANDY *(Canada)*

One wintry day in July, I stood atop a cliff east of Adelaide, along the Great Ocean Drive, overlooking the Southern Sea and the rocks known as the Twelve Apostles. The cold rain was being driven by gale-force winds, and the sea was a turgid white. I took a picture of two pinnacles of rock jutting out from the mainland to create a little harbor and watched the waves seethe in and out of that inlet, crashing with a roar to enormous heights, and then sucked back again into the sea. "That," I said to my companion, "is the postmodern world. And God help the swimmer caught in that turbulence."

It is easy to imagine that the chaos emerging in the world today is simply caused by cultural shifts. Like those two jutting pinnacles of rock, once solid culture is being battered, eroded, and undermined beneath our feet. This turgid sea, however, is not just an accident. We are not simply in a dire *predicament* from which there is no easy escape. The turgidity of our lives is being driven by wind and current. It is Spirit that is actually creating the perfect storm. It is Spirit that is causing the waves to beat against the cultural landscape. What we are experiencing is not simply a *predicament*, but it is a *judgment*. I do not mean some divine vengeance against the moral or spiritual mistakes that we have made. This judgment is more fundamental than that. It is the inevitability of fate that is grinding away at our grandiose claims for autonomy. It is Spirit rising up, swelling up, and raging up to reshape our proud constructions of life. Existence is, and always has been, a perilous and fragile balance between Spirit and culture. That which we have denied for too long, Spirit has made undeniable. We exist between the devil and the deep blue sea. At certain times in history, the stark truth is revealed with utmost clarity.

We are caught in the crunch between Spirit and culture. It isn't the first time. It won't be the last time. The Spirit is in the storm. Indeed, the Spirit is the cause of the storm. The better faith understands what culture is doing, and what Spirit is doing, the clearer faith reveals how to endure until calmer, quieter days. There must be something more that we can do than just keeping our options open, gritting our teeth, clutching tradition, letting go luggage, and whistling in the wind. And there is.

## What Is Culture Doing to Us?

Culture is that complicated mess of human invention that we have fabricated over the centuries to create the illusion of eternity. Because we have been relatively successful controlling our future, we tend to assume we can *absolutely* control our future if we can just educate, assimilate, and coordinate people effectively. Unfortunately, culture is a projection not only of our conscious skills and noble sentiments but also of our unconscious sins and ignoble selfishness. Like Frankenstein, it breaks away from its masters with a mind of its own. What is culture doing to us that is precipitating this perfect storm?

### *Mass Migrations*

We are experiencing the movement of large bodies of people such as the world has never seen. It is akin to the latter stages of the Roman Empire, but faster and more extensive as it encompasses the entire globe. In part, this is the result of a world at peace. We pay for our very success. It is possible for large numbers of people to move in relative safety and optimism from overcrowded places. The number of legal and illegal immigrants relocating for a higher standard of living is staggering. Also in part, this is a result of a world at war. We pay for our tragic failure. It is necessary for large numbers of people to flee rapidly from very dangerous situations. The actual number of refugees is also staggering. We tend to count only the officially declared refugees seeking asylum in neutral countries, but there are many more unofficial refugees running to relatives, religious churches and shrines, or to any slum that provides a bit of anonymity.

This intersection of cultures is so sudden, and so extensive, that it overwhelms the ability of government, business, health care, social services, and religious institutions to manage it. They cannot be educated, assimilated, or coordinated fast enough—and many of them resist the idea that they need to be educated, assimilated, and coordinated in the first place. Resentment increases. Bigotry flourishes.

This rise of bigotry is a key element in the perfect storm as it is precipitated by culture. This is not just the racism or cultural stereotyping that infects all sectors of society, blocking "undesirables" from jobs, housing, medicine, travel, and basic human rights. It cannot simply be countered by affirmative action. This bigotry is the larger context of incivility that has transformed culture from civilization to uncivilization. It is not just that people respect some people and not other people, but that people do not believe in respectability at all. Once the principle is lost, people respect no one but themselves, and in the end, not even themselves.

### *Economic Slavery*

We are experiencing widespread economic slavery in which the seemingly rich and the desperately poor all participate. If global uncivilization has created a free-for-all competition for limited resources, then power and wealth tend to accrue to fewer and fewer people. This is exponential, not just incremental. The power of a few wealthy people, working together, increases their combined ability to control by a factor of ten or more.

Inevitably, mere nations must fall victim to the expansion of such slavery. Elected, appointed, or inherited, the state cannot even protect its own interests against better organized, faster moving, more heavily financed multinational oligarchies. I deliberately avoid the term *corporations* as it is misleading. Corporations working within the law have a vested interest in the well-being of employees, the nurture of volunteers, and the preservation of the state. Multinational oligarchies do not. Their interest is control, plain and simple, and they rely on rhetoric and marketing to keep the slaves in line. Viewed in this light, international terrorism and multinational financing are just competitors.

The perfect storm that is partially precipitated by culture is not really based on war or violence. It is based on unlimited and effectively managed credit. Masters create environments that simply cannot support quality living, and then advance wealth to reshape those environments. Then they charge interest either in coin or blood, with the veiled threat that anything less than obedience will result in cessation of investments and a return to despair. The great goal of sustainable communities is celebrated by master and slave alike. As the perfect storm grows, what are missing are *debt-free* sustainable communities.

### *Commodity Environments*

We are experiencing environmental crises with a frequency and magnitude as never before. This is not news, although beyond popular recognition of global warming, destruction of rain forests, and so on, there are innumerable hidden stories of species extinctions, local pollutions, and secondhand health issues. The perfect storm is not really caused by these crises, but by the pervasive attitude of greed that lies behind them. Culture continues to treat environments as commodities to be used, manipulated, harvested, and consumed.

The persistent attitude of culture is that misguided engineering got us into this situation, but better engineering can get us out of it. All we need is more research and development. This scientistic perversion of genuine science cannot really be blamed on the Enlightenment. No one can blame the present predicament on advances in biology, geology, astronomy, and physics that have advanced public health and human understanding from the dark ages. No, the attitude that manipulates the environment like a commodity stems from the industrialization of the nineteenth century that devalued people and nature as fuel for machines.

The perfect storm is precipitated by our obsession with, and dependence upon, fossil fuels. The obsession is more profound than simply diminishing reserves of oil, gas, and coal. These symbolize something more. They symbolize the very identity of industrialized modernity. Nature has become something to be consumed—devoured, digested, eliminated, and forgotten. More profoundly, labor has become something to be consumed, be they workers, middle managers, or even executives. Everyone is expendable for the profitability of the machine. This is something science never intended or anticipated. We always knew that a little knowledge can be a dangerous thing. We discovered that a lot of knowledge can be an even more dangerous thing.

### *Relational Reductionism*

We are experiencing the reduction of human relationships to the lowest common denominator of sexual interaction and legal entanglement. On the one hand, the heart and soul that render friendship and intimacy profound, joyous, and unpredictable are being reduced to mere gratification of desire. On the other hand, the fidelity and sacrifice that make friendship and intimacy lasting and reliable are being reduced to legal definitions of partnership and marriage that can be manipulated or broken at will.

It is difficult to know whether this reductionism is inspired by media (music, movies, novels, and so on), or whether media is simply reflecting what is happening in culture. Regardless, the increasing incivility of culture is debasing relationships. One can point to international sexual exploitation of children and women, but fundamental relational reductionism is more pervasive. It is visible in the daily victimizations and abuses that we now pass over as normal in daily living. Chronic loss of self-esteem is feeding a rise in physical and emotional violence in schools, businesses, and homes.

Relational reductionism is yet another piece of the perfect storm that is the undoing of civilization. William Wilberforce (whose work in the social maelstrom of the late eighteenth century led to the abolition of the slave trade in Britain in 1807) might preach again for a "reformation of manners."[1] This is a different kind of social conscience that has less to do with public policy and everything to do with how human beings treat other human beings on a daily basis. We no longer converse. We confront.

### *Spiritual Trivialization*

We are experiencing a trivialization of spirituality. In one sense, pagan cultures of antiquity would feel quite at home in the modern world.[2] They would see gods and goddesses, manipulations of divinity, and superstitious rites and rituals remarkably akin to their own. Yet in another sense, ancient pagans would be embarrassed by the triviality and shallowness of spirituality today. It is but a shadow of real paganism. It contains all of the selfishness to manipulate the gods for personal benefits, but none of the awe before the holy. It makes a profit on amulets, dream catchers, and ritual prostitution, but elicits none of the courage and nobility that rages against fate.

Spiritual trivialization is cowardice made sacred. It is the convenience of the church. It is religion as a hobby, as a sociological study, and as an idiosyncrasy of humanity. Professors study it, and then quarrel over tenure. Businessmen dabble in it, and then cheat on their income tax. Ordinary people sacrifice to it, dance in it, and pledge money for it, and then play lotteries. All the New Age crystals, Wiccan rituals, yoga spas, modern-day prayers to Thor (and yes, pseudo-Christian, Gnostic praise services) all lead to nothing. No one risks much, dares much, or sacrifices much. Martyrdom is considered a tactical mistake.

The perfect storm reaches its peak of destructive power because genuine spirituality, that last stand against evil, has gone soft. I do not mean religious militancy (which is really economic slavery in disguise), but authentic spiritual discipline. It doesn't even have to be Christian, although anyone familiar with Jesus would know it ought to be Christian. It just needs to be humble before the Holy, compassionate toward the downtrodden, and courageous enough to risk everything for the sake of justice.

This is what culture is doing to us. Our own creation seems to be running amok, but in reality it is only doing extremely well what sinners deep in their twisted minds wanted in the first place. Yet what if there is something more to the perfect storm than culture gone crazy? What if there is an unseen power of Spirit that is pushing culture to the limits of destructiveness in order to purge humanity of its deeper selfishness?

## What Is Spirit Doing to Us?

In the perspective of faith, we suddenly realize that it is not culture alone that is rolling us about in the waves of change. We might indeed cry out: "Woe is me! The godly people have perished from the earth, and there is none upright. The day of their punishment has come; now their confusion is at hand! But as for me, I will look to the Lord and I will wait for the God of my salvation!"[3] There is something more to this perfect storm than meets the eye. Spirit is in it.

Our situation brings to mind Luke's peculiar view of Spirit and culture in the Acts of the Apostles. The story that begins with Pentecost ends in shipwreck, just as our modern story seems to begin with Enlightenment and end in disaster. The apostle Paul is normally an emotional man, but he is remarkably calm and dispassionate during the storm at sea. Somehow it is all part of a larger divine plan, and he submits to being blown by the wind. What, then, is Spirit doing to us?

### *Redefining Home*

Spirit is driving us to redefine home. Culture may be about mass migrations, but Spirit is about rethinking our origins, identity, and destiny. Contrary to popular belief, home is *not* where the heart is. Home is where the soul flies. It is not a location, a language, or a set of behavioral expectations. It is the spiritual womb from which we emerged, from which we carry our spiritual genetic signature, and to which we return for solace or salvation. Home is a relationship that we have with that which is ultimate and absolute in our lives.

We are slowly discovering that portability is the crucial test of our identity. We must be able to take value and meaning on the road. If our spiritual compass depends on sacred space, or sacred place, or sacred things, we will quickly lose our bearings. To what do we turn for strength in stressful times of trouble and doubt? These are the convictions that give hope in the immediacy of our anxiety. We cannot put anxiety on hold while we journey back to our place of origin. That place must be within our own soul.

This is a huge challenge for modern people who have become addicted to stability. Yes, small portions of the world have been prone to instability, but we always considered that to be abnormal. For the first time in a long time (although there have been other times!), we have been forced to realize what prophets from all religions have always maintained, namely, that instability is normal for human existence. This is the root source of the culture of fear that has emerged in the new millennium in Europe, North America, Australia, and countless villages and neighborhoods around the world. Instability was something that happened over there, and suddenly it is the norm everywhere. Therefore, we must look for stability within our souls. We are at best sojourners in any given place and time.

Spirit challenges all nationalisms as inherently addictive, self-destructive behavior patterns that are often denied or even ridiculed, but which grip our hearts and rob us of hope. They tempt us to define ourselves by our origins. Spirit draws us to redefine ourselves by our destinies. We are not defined by where we came from; we are defined by where we are going. That destiny has little to do with geography and everything to do with spirituality. The problem is that once nationalism, tribalism, and all the other isms are removed, we are left naked and hopeless. Yet until such addictions are removed, we are unable to peer deeper into the soul to discover a more ultimate concern and a more absolute acceptance. Spirit would bring us home by bringing home to us—an acceptance that is portable and lasting.

*Challenging Fatalism*

Spirit is awakening our thirst for autonomy. Culture presses upon us economic slavery, but Spirit lifts us from sullen obedience to assert our independence. We are not doomed to dependency. There is another way to assert ourselves and take authority for our lives. Our situation is akin to the shattering of feudalism in fourteenth-century Europe and the rise of the middle-class entrepreneur. We do not have to be held in thrall to political principalities; we can discern, design, implement, and evaluate our own choices without having to ask the permission of a master. Yet it is no accident that the liberation of Europe from feudalism in the fourteenth century was only accomplished in an era of plague, natural disaster, and social upheaval. Spirit uses the perfect storm to set people free to take responsibility for their own lives.

The spiritual challenge to fatalism goes far deeper than simple economics. The chronic experience of uncertainty in the midst of the perfect storm of today is due as much to the working of Spirit as to the demise of confidence in scientific discovery, political will, or military security. The certainties of the past have created fatalism about the future. It was at once comforting and hopeless. Humanity itself became the price of confidence. Health, harmony, and security could seemingly only be won at the cost of compassion, creativity, and freedom. Now that this false confidence has been shattered, there is fresh opportunity for personal empowerment. The individual can emerge from being dominated to take full and radical responsibility for living.

The great irony is that when Spirit challenges fatalism, so many people choose to resist it. Rather than accept the risks and responsibilities of freedom, they long to return to slavery. The perfect storm is like the melee of prisoners suddenly and unexpectedly released from prison. At first their behavior is anarchic, even violent, because they hardly know what to do with their liberation. Some press forward, accepting the risks and responsibilities of freedom; some retreat backward, longing for the security that the narrow boxes of scientific method, political authority, and police security, or religious dogma could provide. We see today this anarchy of visions. Will people sacrifice even their humanity to return to the harmony and security of a life trapped and enclosed by genetic engineering, political totalitarianism, religious fundamentalism, social prejudice, and military intimidation? Or will people risk their comforts to take responsibility for living and align themselves with a higher purpose for humanity? What we have learned in the perfect storm is that this choice has been taken out of our hands. Spirit will drive humanity forward.

### *Facing Death*

Spirit is forcing us to face the inevitability of our death. It is not just our death. It is your death, my death, that confronts us in the environmental crises that befall us. No corner of the earth is immune. What is new about that? The environment is always changing, natural disasters have always occurred, accidents have always been random, and aging has always been inexorable. What is new is the length to which contemporary people have strived to avoid, delay, and ultimately deny the inevitability of death. The more technologically advanced we have become, the more the deception can be perpetuated. We live in the illusion that there is always a health cure waiting to be discovered or a social service ready to rescue us. There is a lottery to be won, a switch to be turned on, or a dike that will hold. But in the perfect storm, when the hurricane has landed, and the flood is rising, and the tornado is roaring, and *nothing works*, we are forced to face the truth. We—you, me, children, parents, family, friends—will surely die.

Why should Spirit drive us so pitilessly to face death? It is only in so doing that we feel the absolute threat of meaninglessness. Our first reaction is to flee to old idols or create new religious or quasireligious symbols, and so today we see a resurrection of pagan gods and goddesses, shrines and holy places, but even these are swept away in the collapse of environments. Our next reaction is to flee to education. Our Protestant heritage has encouraged us to believe that if only people were literate, could learn and study, and preach and be preached to, their good sense would prevail, and humanity could survive. Yet the collapse of environments will overwhelm universities and research laboratories, and even the printed pages of a Bible will turn moldy in our dead hands. So our third reaction is to despair. And this is the real reason Spirit drives us to face death, for it is only in facing despair that humanity can find authentic courage, and we can hope to survive the storm.

Facing death is the only way we can make an absolute choice for life. It alone can precipitate the courage to act in spite of death. We can finally, realistically, and courageously focus on what will happen *after* death. What will happen *after* the death of a parent, child, or friend? What will happen *after* the death of cities, nations, and churches? What will happen *after* my own death? When the storm passes, what will be left? What should be left? What will we stake our very lives on in order to make *this particular thing survive*? What is worth the cost of my life? Facing death means recognizing that my obliteration, or the obliteration of even my family, my country, or my culture, is not the end of history. Spirit drives us to recognize that *there is something more*. This greater meaning is not dependent on ego, or the pretensions of ego, we call *heritage*, or even the extension of ego we call *culture*. The discovery of that "something more" is what overcomes despair and meaninglessness.

*Recovering Honor*

Spirit is driving us to recover dignity in our relationships. Culture may have caused us to treat human beings as objects and reduce relationships to the lowest common denominators of sex and victimization, but Spirit challenges us to restore our sense of honor. We are driven to recognize the complexity, fragility, and potential for good within other human beings. We find ways to work in partnership rather than in competition. We negotiate our demands for gratification. We respect the autonomy of the other.

The perfect storm precipitates this possibility to recover honor by revealing the profound loneliness, isolation, or alienation that has been caused by the relational reductionism of culture. This is the leverage point. Loneliness is the inevitable result of consistent relational reductionism, because the objectification of others implies the objectification of oneself. Abuse of others leads inevitably to abuse of self. Society is caught in a vicious cycle of victimization, as people are alternatively, even in the span of fifteen minutes, both victims and victimizers. The resulting loneliness is all the more terrifying, because we all recognize that everyone is as lonely as we are, and everyone is powerless to do anything about it.

The recovery of honor begins with courageous civility. It is the risk of treating others as human beings of intrinsic worth through basic discourse and behavioral habits. It expands through investment of time and money in the emotional maturity and vocational ambitions of the other, even at the cost of self-advancement. It leads to a readiness to sacrifice oneself, even to the point of martyrdom, for the well-being of strangers. Honor is only recovered once principles of truth, beauty, and goodness replace the self-centered relativism of everyday behavior. Spirit drives people in, through, and beyond loneliness that measures others against the demands of self-interest, toward principles that set the standard of a larger consensus.

## Experiencing Incarnation

Spirit makes the infinite transparent to the finite. Even as culture trivializes spirituality, Spirit makes the world (the cosmos) intrinsically sacramental. Even the most trivial object can become symbolic of deeper meaning. Objects may not only remind us of infinite meaning but become portals through which the infinite can touch, shape, and transform everyday existence. Chronological time can be filled with *kairos* moments in which infinite meaning erupts into everyday experience. These are moments of incarnation in which the fullness of the divine and the fullness of humanity merge if only for an instant.

Incarnation may be anticipated prophetically, but it is only experienced apocalyptically. The perfect storm is an apocalyptic experience, in which life is turned upside down and inside out. It is precisely in these times when life is utterly out of control and obviously beyond human management that human spirit and divine spirit connect. It will be intuitive and ecstatic; it may seem emotional and electric; but it will be an overwhelming or deepening experience that changes our lives. There is a reason prophets, monastics, and religious leaders have described the experience of God using metaphors of whirlwind, devouring fire, and abyss—all apocalyptic metaphors similar to perfect storm. These are nonrational encounters with the Holy.

Spirit drives us toward these encounters because only in the extremes of stress can we break through to the depths of peace. Our fear, meaninglessness, loneliness, and anxiety are resolved not in clarity, but in mystery. It is an acceptance that we cannot prove, understand, or even explain. It empowers us to accept ways that we thought impossible in the maelstrom of the storm. This is the paradox of incarnation, and in the depths of this paradox lie the roots of our humanity. Spirit is indeed driving us back to the basics, but these are not fundamentalist dogmas or cultural norms. We get in touch with the foundations of thought and hope that make us what we are.

## How Is the Perfect Storm Reshaping Our Lives?

The perfect storm is caused by the convergence of culture and Spirit. Perhaps it is better to say it is caused by the *confrontation* of culture and Spirit. This has always been true at different periods in history, but today it is happening simultaneously on a global scale. All of us, collectively and cross-culturally, are caught between culture and Spirit.

We may feel at times that we are simply riding out the storm in open waters, but the truth is that we are being reshaped by the storm. The storm is eroding the cultural landscape here and creating new islands and inlets there, so that by the time we reach port once again we will be making landfall in a very different world.

Our initial reaction is that the perfect storm is something that is happening to us, around us, and in spite of us. Then it becomes clear that although culture is out of our control, the cultural trends and upheavals are a direct result of our own decisions and addictions. Our real hope lies in the final awareness that we are not just flotsam and jetsam driven by the power of Spirit. We have an intrinsic connection with Spirit, just as we have an intrinsic connection with culture. In short, as helpless as we often feel, we are not powerless. Caught in the confrontation between culture and Spirit, there are things that we can do, and already we can see how the perfect storm is reshaping our lives.[4]

### *The Quest for Serenity*

Humanity is embarking on a whole new quest for serenity. There is a reason that twelve-step programs are collectively the fastest-growing spirituality in the world today and that the most popular and memorable prayer is the Serenity Prayer. Serenity is the child of courage and wisdom. It is not mere passivity, nor simply a peaceful demeanor, nor just psychological balance, nor some studied indifference to suffering. Serenity is the state of accepting acceptance and of perfect alignment with the will of God. Whether in stability or movement, abundance or want, serenity is the confidence of unity with God. Among all cultures, and hidden within all religious movements, this quest for serenity is capturing public attention and allegiance.

It is partly a result of courage to stand over against the existential anxieties of meaninglessness, loneliness, guilt, fear, and fate. This is a lifestyle discipline. It is a decision, yes, but a decision that is repeated over and over again on a daily and even hourly basis. It is much like a decision for sobriety. The alcoholic does not decide to be sober *forever*, but *only one day at a time*. Even so, one decides courageously to stand against existential anxiety one day at a time, or one relationship at a time, or one refugee camp at a time, or one crisis at a time.

Cumulatively, it is a lifestyle of courage. It is a practice of self-discipline, as one resists temptation to despair.

It is also a result of wisdom that measures the limits of expectation. Wisdom is a form of radical honesty. It does not deny the self, but recognizes the limits of selfhood. It acknowledges the boundaries of what the ego cannot do and guides the development of community partnerships and support in order to go beyond what the self can accomplish. Wisdom goes further. It faces the limitations of what even networks of relationships can achieve and surrenders one's destiny to a Higher Power. The essence of courage is self-assurance, but the essence of wisdom is humility.

Together these paradoxical forces shape the experience of serenity. It may be hard to sustain consistently through the mass migrations of body and mind, but the quest for it dominates human consciousness.[5]

*The Quest for Credibility*

Humanity is embarking on a new quest for credibility. There is a reason the public has a penchant for idolizing heroes. Our heroes may be as diverse as cultic leaders, Catholic saints, rock musicians, and television or movie stars, but beneath the often-shallow equation of success and spirituality lies a deep hunger for credible leadership.[6] Credibility is a combination of clear vision, high integrity, mentoring ability, and team participation. Credibility is a rare and precious thing. It takes years to earn credibility and only minutes to lose it. The fantasy of television and film can compress time, and the artificiality of the press can distort facts, making Hollywood personalities and political figures seem more credible than they really are. Indeed, the very liturgy of the church can make religious leaders more credible than they really are.

The gullibility of the public to slick marketing belies a more canny intuition of the truth. They seek leaders who can model and mentor a positive future, holistic health, a moral compass, empathy for individual context and yearning, and readiness to cooperate across cultures and public sectors. The challenge is both to model *and* to mentor. Demonstrate and share, evoke and provoke, reveal and train what it means to be healthy, moral, adaptive, cooperative . . . and aligned to a positive vision that is greater than oneself. There may be a chronic cynicism about ever finding such a leader, but humanity as a whole is starved for credibility, and people are seeking it more earnestly than ever before.

If economic slavery is a product of overextended credit, then the only way to overcome resignation and despair is to discern overarching credibility. The recovery of credibility for global leadership requires more than debt forgiveness. It requires debt assumption. It is the willingness of affluent leaders to assume the debt, shoulder the burden, and walk in companionship with the poor stranger. It is the readiness to do more than sympathize with suffering, but to go further to share the suffering, so that leaders can lead from within the very midst of humanity who are broken, lost, lonely, anxious, fearful, and victimized and guide the public to the other side of the storm.

### *The Quest for Heaven*

Humanity is embarking on a new quest for life—after life. There is a reason that people are increasingly interested in the supernatural, and especially obsessed with the devil. Heaven is a mystery best defined by what it is not. Descriptions of heaven have long been abandoned by the skepticism of modernity, so that even to speculate about heaven is immediately regarded as shameful, immature, and downright stupid. So instead, we paint elaborate and wildly speculative pictures of what we abhor, afraid to even name or hope for what we really desire.

Spirit drives us to desire heaven, because without it there is nothing left but death. Heaven is not only the desire for an ultimate perfection and joy, in which we can participate wholly, unreservedly, and forever, but it is also the desire for ultimate accountability. Human justice, no matter how vigorously pursued, has no lasting comfort unless it is rooted in apocalyptic expectation. If there is no ultimate accountability, there is no accountability that is really worth pursuing. If there is no ultimate acceptance, there is no solace that is really worth seeking.

The modern accusation is that heaven is a psychological trick rather than an intrinsic ontological expectation, as if the desire for heaven is some bourgeois tactic for passivity. On the contrary, postmodern people are discovering that the desire for heaven is a tactic for revolution. The mere promise sustains the struggle for justice and sends martyrs to their deaths singing. People are awakening to the realization that, contrary to modern medical opinion, there is something radically *unnatural* about death. It is illogical, out of alignment, and incompatible with life. The greatest deception, and the dirtiest trick, of modernity has been the illusion that there *shouldn't be* a life after death. Of course there should! It makes perfect sense that there should! The shame of believing in heaven is gradually being washed away by the perfect storm, and people are allowed to have visions of eternity.

### *The Quest for Absolutes*

Humanity is embarking on a new quest for paradigms of the good, the true, and the beautiful. This claim contradicts many contemporary descriptions of the radical relativism of postmodern people, and it is true that humanity caught in the perfect storm renounces the absolute claims of any dogma, doctrine, tradition, institution, or even scientific proof. Modernity was lived in a partial relativism, in which nothing was absolute except ego. Postmodernity now questions even the absolute claims of ego. Even *I myself* am not absolute to myself. Our absolute relativism reveals our conviction in absolutes beyond absolutes, a God above gods, to which everything including ego is relative.

Yet this absolute is hidden. Every attempt to express it, conceptualize it, draw it, or define it immediately obscures it. We can't even talk about it or describe it without losing it. Look at it directly and it disappears, and yet it reappears out of the corner of our eyes, in the peripheral vision of our souls, and in the gasp of what remains unsaid. Everything is relative because it is there, and if it were not there then some limited god or ego would claim to be absolute, only to be violently *relative-ized* tomorrow. It is this inevitable shattering of *all* claims to ultimacy that implies to postmodern imagination an absolute reality beyond conceptualization.

It is our intuition that this unknown God somehow is the key to perfection, because we are convinced that everything else is mere approximation. All religions are *relatively* true, because there is some hidden absolute truth to which they point. All art is *relatively* beautiful, because there is something absolutely beautiful from which it borrows. All relationships are *relatively* good, because there is some lover who is *perfectly good*. People move from perspective to perspective, expression to expression, and relationship to relationship. They cannot settle for an approximation or be content with imperfection, but are restlessly seeking that which is precious and hidden.

The remnants of modernity will ask, "Must this absolute be personified?" Such a question reveals the dualism of industrialized modernity that treats heart and soul and all those metaphors to describe personhood as somehow less real than facts, genetics, and actuarial statistics. Postmodern people caught in the terror and urgency of the perfect storm will ask back, "How can this absolute not be personified?" For if it is not the ultimate perfection of heart and soul as well, it cannot be ultimate in any meaningful sense at all.

### *The Quest for the Paradoxical Presence of God*

Humanity is embarking on a new quest for the paradoxical presence of God. There is a reason why so much media attention is being given to the historicity or nonhistoricity of Jesus of Nazareth. Behind all the rival claims and archaeological debates to support or debunk traditional assumptions about Jesus, there is a deeper hunger for the immediacy of God. There is a longing for the impossible, namely, the *touch* of the *Holy*. We yearn for the absolute to be immediate, and for that which is beyond imagination and definition to touch our brow, wipe our tear, or echo our laughter.

This quest is not limited to a specific established religion or religious institution. It is visible more broadly in the literature, music, and visual art that are global and cross-cultural phenomena—and specifically in the *fantasy* literature, *popular* music, and *urban street* art that aims at ecstasy. The emerging human passion to be beside oneself reveals the yearning to be beyond oneself, to escape human limitations just enough to touch, or be touched by, the Holy. The fact that there is no consensus about the nature of that holy grail is unimportant. The conviction is all that matters.

Yet there is a profound undercurrent of anxiety in this quest, and the resolution of this anxiety personally and collectively may determine if, when, and how humanity emerges from the perfect storm in which we are caught. Is the Hidden Holy indifferent to humanity or does it care about us? To the modern mind, predisposed to limit truth to verifiability, the best one can say is maybe. There is plenty of evidence that the

Hidden Holy is indeed indifferent to the mechanics of life, yet there is growing evidence that it reaches out to touch our fingertips. The more we become unclear about what even constitutes evidence, the more we contemplate the courageous irrationality of a leap of faith.

## What Will Spiritual Leaders Do?

I recall again my journey between Adelaide and Melbourne. There I am standing on the cliff above the Southern Sea in a raging winter gale, watching the surf churn around the Twelve Apostles. At one time, these pillars of hardened stone might have been a bulwark against the raging sea, protecting the cultural landscape, and even providing islands of rescue and safety to storm-tossed sailors. Now they are eroded and crumbling. Only a handful of the original Twelve Apostles are left, and one toppled over even in the past three years since I was there. I recall my words: "That," I said to my companion, "is the postmodern world. And God help the swimmer caught in that turbulence." So, standing as we are on the cliffs of Christendom and the crumbling edges of culture, what exactly are we to do?

This is the religious and cultural situation as I have described it here. The perfect storm is created by the clash of culture and Spirit, and we are caught in the middle. Yet we are not merely passive. We have embarked on a new quest for meaning.

| Culture | Caught In Between | Spirit |
|---|---|---|
| Mass migrations | The quest for serenity | Redefining home |
| Economic slavery | The quest for credibility | Challenging fatalism |
| Commodity | The quest for heaven | Facing death environments |
| Relational reductionism | The quest for absolutes | Recovering honor |
| Spiritual trivialization | The quest for the paradoxical presence of God | Experiencing incarnation |

Lest we think our situation is historically unique, it may be helpful to reread the address given by my mentor, Paul Tillich, to the fiftieth church congress of the Protestant Episcopal Church in Indianapolis, Indiana, on May 6, 1942.[7] It is aptly entitled "Storms of Our Times." In the midst of the seething cultural crises and bubbling spiritualities that precipitated the violence that has dogged the twentieth century, Tillich asks the assembly: "What have we done for the fulfillment of the religious demand in the present world revolution?"[8] Our perfect storm is not something a few leaders have suddenly discovered, nor has it crashed into the cultural landscape without warning. We have seen it from afar. It has arrived. It will get worse before it gets better. It will change our world in a way that renders the social upheavals and national transformations from 1914 to 1945 only the first gusts of wind.

Yet it is unclear whether the church today is any better prepared to guide humanity through the storm than it was sixty-five years ago. In some ways, it is. The church has occasionally and effectively addressed mass migrations, economic slavery, commodity environments, relational reductionism, and spiritual trivialization—and sporadically led the way in redefining home, challenging fatalism, facing death, recovering honor, and experiencing incarnation. In many ways, however, the established church has shared the denial of other public sectors toward these issues, and allowed itself to be sidetracked by things that are fundamentally irrelevant to the five great quests of humanity today.

Spiritual leaders should lead the quests of humanity. There is every reason to think that explicitly Christian leaders can and should lead all five of these quests. Who would be better positioned to respond to the crisis of being caught between culture and Spirit than people who believe in Jesus Christ, fully human and fully divine, infinite mystery, but crucial to salvation? The challenge, frankly, seems to surpass the abilities of current churchy institutions to call, equip, and send Christian people into the storm. At best, we seem only able to equip and send Christian people to face a stiff breeze.

- The only people who can lead the quest for serenity are people who have experienced it. They are people who have already redefined home for a world in which physical, mental, and emotional migration is the norm.

- The only people who can lead the quest for credibility are people who have already submitted to radical accountability. They are people who have liberated themselves from slavery only to assume the burdens of the world.

- The only people who can lead the quest for heaven are people who have tasted it. They are people who are willing to take the vows of true asceticism, reducing their standards of luxury, and even facing death, for the sake of hope in the world.

- The only people who can lead the quest for absolutes are people who honor strangers. They are people who surrender personal, congregational, and denominational ego to the unconditional demands of God's mission and who align their behavior to a higher standard of morality, honesty, and compassion.

- The only people who can lead the quest for the paradoxical presence of God are people who really have been touched by the holy. They are people who know Jesus, having merged, united, and connected with the healing, guiding, vindicating, encouraging, modeling, and transforming power of God.

Do these leaders exist? Yes, but perhaps in unlikely places, with unlikely credentials, associating with unlikely people. Perfect storms test the mettle of the admirals, captains, crew, and passengers on any ship—and reveal the truth about the lifeguards, lighthouse keepers, swimmers, and sunbathers on any beach.

I hear the echo of Tillich's last sentence in his 1942 address "Storms of Our Times." He was preoccupied by the war and its aftermath, but with an eye to uncover the real motivations of conflict and the future implications of peace. It is not hard to paraphrase. "What hope do we have for a constructive answer to these . . . questions? I cannot answer . . . but what I do know is that if the meaning of the [perfect storm] is not understood and accepted, night will fall over us for generations."[9]

CHAPTER TWELVE

# Celestial Storms: Dreaming of Novae

PETER J. WALKER *(United States)*

Christianity is staring out a dripping porthole and the sea looks rough. That's an understatement that even perfect storm belies. We may not have reached the *final frontier*, but few would argue that we are rocketing into *undiscovered country*. We are the voyagers who boldly go—I feel like Chicken Little because, by God, the sky is falling! Perhaps we carry the legacy of Noah, watching as "the floodgates of the heavens were opened."[1] It's raining for the first time again.

The other day I found myself chatting with an agnostic friend. Chris was ranting about Western imperialism and "the geopolitical hammer of American justice." As he thoughtfully rolled a homemade cigarette in his hand, he suggested that U.S. foreign policy functioned a lot like a religious structure. "You mean like Christianity?" I tried to clarify. "No. Christianity itself is harmless," Chris answered. *Harmless*. Not *out of touch*, not *corrupt*, not *arrogant* or *dangerous*. Just harmless, like a ferocious toddler or a frolicsome puppy. We don't matter as much as we think we do—or thought we did. The weather fronts in this perfect storm we face are more unusual than the cyclical El Niño fare we're used to. We need to do more than open our umbrellas (for example, add drums and electric guitars to our praise music). There's a foreign quality to all this—something humans haven't seen before. The initial indicators of this storm feel like solar winds, blowing gusts of post-Christendom apathy down into our stratosphere. This apathy doesn't waste its time reacting or even responding to Christianity because it doesn't think about Christianity. We don't blip the radar. We're harmless. Yes there are still post-Christian hostilities toward Christianity here and there—people who have been burned, wounded, or are simply fed up with media portrayals and picket-sign culture wars. (It's hard to fault them for that: we have not behaved well.) Anti-Christian sentiment tends to open up great inroads for repentance, humility, and reconciliation. At the very least, anti-Christian rhetoric gives us the chance to turn the other cheek and love our enemies.

When Jonah saw the storm he knew in his heart that it was his own creation: "Pick me up and throw me into the sea . . . and it will become calm."[2] Oh, that we were so brave! We find the answers less clear in post-*Christendom* than in post-*Christian*, because Christendom pertains largely to culture, not spirit. The spirit shift happened some time ago, and we weren't paying attention. Now, the whole culture is shifting, and we can't ignore it. The outer accoutrements of the Western church are decomposing, and we're asking why the world doesn't care.

Not long ago I dreamed that the church had finally had enough of me! Two pastor friends of mine approached, saying, "Peter, we're through with your indignant ranting. It's time for you to leave." They threw me out of Christendom. The pain of such rejection cut right to my guts. Countless times I had longed to walk away from the church without looking back (to look back might have turned me into a salty pillar of modernity). But I had always stayed out of love for the Body of Christ. In the dream, I left broken and dejected. All around me, beautiful stars fell from the sky, exploding like fireworks against the black space of night. I woke up and found myself warmly entrenched in Christianity's safe organizational structure. The falling stars were the only true part of my dream: somewhere off in unseen infinity an explosive celestial storm was brewing.

Supernovae are stellar explosions that can occur at the death of stars. The star may either cease to generate energy and implode too rapidly—resulting in a black hole, vacuuming light and matter at an inescapable rate—or it may become so cosmically obese and overgrown that it no longer remains stable. Viewers millions of light years away can see the mammoth destruction unfold like a televangelistic nightmare—big bang. Like a congregation spiraling in turf war, a star will collapse in on itself before it goes supernova. This enormous ball of heat and light and energy grows erratic and may shrink down to a fraction of its once grand scale. In this way, the crashing sun looks rather sorry. It becomes darker and denser than it has ever been before. Its nuclear fuel is exhausted—nothing left to burn, too much negative energy. The star implodes.

Compared to the memory of what once was, a star in this process looks to be an astrological failure, no more prophetic radiance to Magi below. As the light goes out, heat fades; size and shape are all but lost. The blackness of space looms all around and the light of other stars shines only faintly in the distance. Debris and refuse with no former connection to this star are suddenly pulled in by the swelling vortex—particles from all over space accommodated and absorbed. Imperceptibly, the vacuum of this star grows too strong and the tiny nucleus too dense. The star's core is loaded with neutrons—little subatomic particles with no electrical charge. If there are enough of them, they stop the continued collapse and the star explodes. It *explodes*! Light flashes, heat emanates and spreads—talk about a perfect storm. This one fills a galaxy.

Reborn as a nebula cloud, everything that previously existed as a star will be suddenly, radically transformed. The old dying sun gives way to a new, bright, expanding cloud of heavenly gas and particles. Delicately, it will spread its way through space in pink and purple hues and yellow tracers. Everything in space that comes in contact with the cloud may pass through unharmed but for shimmering wisps of gas that cling tightly, resonating a halo effect, glowing.

But if those neutrons in the star don't do their job and reverse the collapse, a star's core completely falls into itself—black hole. With black holes, the solar casualty only gives way to further desecration: ultimate gravity pulls everything around itself into nothingness incarnate. Not even light escapes.

Jesus Christ has called us to be neutrons who stop the black-hole collapse of the Body. We must live as those tiny particles with no electrically charged egos getting in the way of God's perfect postmodern storm: a supernova right here on planet Earth. When we do things like defend cultural norms or political structures, we begin taking on electrical charge. We start wiring this Christian star for self-destruct. The beatitude life of Jesus discharges all that electrical junk and stops the vortex from forming.

> Blessed are the poor in spirit,
> for theirs is the kingdom of heaven.
> Blessed are those who mourn,
> for they will be comforted.
> Blessed are the meek,
> for they will inherit the earth.
> Blessed are those who hunger and thirst for righteousness,
> for they will be filled.
> Blessed are the merciful,
> for they will be shown mercy.
> Blessed are the pure in heart,
> for they will see God.
> Blessed are the peacemakers,
> for they will be called sons of God.
> Blessed are those who are persecuted because of righteousness,
> for theirs is the kingdom of heaven.[3]

It's hard to fight culture wars when we're poor in spirit, merciful, and making peace. It's easy to redream our ecclesiology, our theology, our soteriology, and the beautiful Creation we inhabit when we're pure, meek, hungry, and thirsty for righteousness. Can we trust the Holy Spirit to lead, rather than ourselves? We don't need an ark this time to stay out of choppy waters—we don't need a NASA spacesuit, either. In this unexplored atmosphere, the only way to fail the mission is to protect ourselves from it.

> For whoever wants to save his life will lose it, but whoever loses his life for me will find it.[4]

Supernovae are rare (occurring only once in fifty years in a galaxy the size of the Milky Way) and few humans witness one with their own eyes. In spite of the odds, these explosions are crucial to enriching the galaxy with necessary elements. They are part of the universe's self-renewal process: subsequent shockwaves can actually trigger the formation of new stars.

So the choice is left to us. The church is shrinking. The Christianity of yesterday is dimming. The bright stars of Protestantism and Evangelicalism are in jeopardy. Even the nascent protostar of Pentecostalism fades into the shared plasma of its older siblings. It's astronomical reality. Close your eyes if you want to—the sun is still wasting away. But the glory of the Son may be rising. Even as Christendom itself feels the pangs of decay, a chain of new and vibrant elements are in place that could *explode* in a brilliant, electrifying supernova.

The church can be reborn amid the unprecedented storms it faces (those storms, terrestrial and extraterrestrial). But be warned: ours is a God not only of the past but of the future. When this rebirth happens, it won't look like the church as we have known it. We are not in a world as we have known it. Its presencc will be gentle and broad and effervescent. Not contextualized, but consecrated. Not revived, but redreamed. This redreamed church will reach into our hearts instead of our heads only. It will change our realities—not simply our ideas. It will rekindle our relationships instead of our fanaticism. And we will glow in the light of a living God: Jesus Christ, the star who exploded throughout our world and Who still desires to light our way into tomorrow.

> I, Jesus, have sent my angel to give you this testimony for the churches. I am the Root and the Offspring of David, and the bright Morning Star. The Spirit and the bride say, "Come!" And let him who hears say, "Come!" Whoever is thirsty, let him come; and whoever wishes, let him take the free gift of the water of life.[5]

CHAPTER THIRTEEN

# Manual and Chart Notes for Stormy Seas

LEONARD SWEET *(United States)*

*The sea gives amply and takes amply*

ANCIENT SAILOR'S PROVERB

One of the few places the Second Testament talks about leadership (the Bible is much more prone to talk about *followers*hip) is in Paul's listing of the charisms of the Body of Christ in 1 Corinthians 12:28. One particular "gift of the Spirit" in this list is represented by the Greek word, *kubernao*. Most translators use words like *administration* or *governance* or *leadership* to convey the meaning of this word. But *kubernao* is a nautical term that literally means *helmsmanship* or *steersmanship*.[1] Biblical scholar Anthony C. Thiselton says that the concept of leadership here conveys a pilot's "ability to formulate strategies" especially "through the choppy waters of strife and status seeking."[2]

The church needs pilots who can steer the ship through stormy seas. So how best to weather the perfect storm? How best to captain the ship through troubled waters?

One way *not* to handle the perfect storm is to complain about the weather. You don't go through any storm, much less a perfect one, in the fetal position, whimpering and whining and wringing your hands. It does no good to harrumph and snort about how awful things are. When asked how to learn the virtue of patience, Rabi'a, a Muslim who lived a thousand years ago in Baghdad, replied: "Stop complaining."

If you put life on hold while waiting for the weather to break, you could spend your whole life on hold. Adjust yourself accordingly, knowing that one day the weather will break. When you're tempted to yammer and yell when storms come to pass, make these four words your mantra: it came to pass. The storm may last days, months, years, decades, but the storm will leave as it came, with almost supernatural suddenness.

Rather than waste time in weather bashing, invest yourself in weather reports: take changing phenomena and work them into a prognosis for the days and weeks to come.

*The pessimist complains about the wind;*
*the optimist expects it to change;*
*the realist adjusts the sails.*

WILLIAM ARTHUR WARD[3]

Another way *not* to handle a storm is to blame God for sending it your way. I love the stormy night story of Saint Teresa of Avila (1515–1582). Her coach overturned, landing herself and her sisters in the mud. She is said to have prayed, "if this is the way you treat your friends, Lord, it is no wonder you have so few." It's a prayer worth saying and saving, but it's a prayer that doesn't make weathering storms any easier. God has fair-weather friends aplenty.

A third way *not* to handle the perfect storm is crisis management and risk assessment. The notion that any storm can be managed smacks of ambitions both soppy and pretentious. To aspire for any kind of control or cleanup when you're holding on for dear life as Mother Nature does a demolition job is delusional. Damage will be done, and dust will settle; damages cannot be managed, swept away, or swept under the carpet. Sometimes even prophets have to live through what they foretell: Jeremiah warned of the doom of his city, and when it was laid siege he joined the Hebrew people in their slide to the depths, in spite of his warning. Pleasing God is not always pleasing.

*You lift me up on the wind, you make me ride on it, and you toss me about in the roar of the storm.*

JOB 30:22

The fourth way *not* to handle the perfect storm is to spend your time fighting with other passengers on the boat. Many Christians are like passengers fighting with each other over who's got the better table and better place at the pool, while there's a storm outside ready to capsize the boat.

Here are five things for helmsmen to keep in mind when navigating the perfect storm. Each one is at odds with common sense. Each one is counterintuitive in its own way.

## 1. Lift Anchor and Put Out into the Deep

*The shore is safer, Abiah [Root], but I love to buffet the sea—I can count the bitter wrecks here in these pleasant waters, and hear the murmuring winds, but oh, I love the danger!*

EMILY DICKINSON[4]

In times of storm, the shore is *not* safer (Emily Dickinson notwithstanding). In fact, the shore is the most dangerous place to be in the midst of a storm. Hugging harbors leaves a church in the lurch. A church in the dock is a church in lockdown.

The root meaning of the verb *to forgive* is "to let go, to cease to harbor." What are you harboring at great personal cost? It is as dangerous for you to harbor in your personal life as in your church life. A fort fortifies nothing and no one.[5]

Fundamentalism is a harboring response to the perfect storm. A lot of people make fun of bubble-headed, Bible-belted, Qur'an-kissing "fundies." But they have my sympathy and love. At least they are aware that something is awry[6] and have shunned the wistful, wishful spirituality that has gripped much of the church. It is almost as if the enormity of what is happening in our world can only seep into a small part of the church's awareness, the most superficial part, leaving everything else peacefully asleep and dwelling in cloud cuckoo-land. *It's not a storm; just a little shower that needs only an umbrella.*

It is understandable why, in some fishing villages, the houses near the sea face the land, not the water. They are bordered up backwards, with windows and doors facing gardens and greenery toward the land, and with few openings toward the water. "No one who earns his living from the real chaos of the sea would want to look at it as he goes to sleep—no, these squares are defensive only in the mind; in here, it's peace, the female, sex, the wife, domesticity, children, the deep rewards of life. Out there it's . . . ."[7]

Osama bin Laden's indictment of the West for the spiritual vacuum at the heart of its materialistic culture is searing. Fundamentalism's diagnosis is right. The world is raging with gale-force winds and waves. But their prescription is faulty: hug the harbor and wait out the storm.

Fundamentalism is a Thomas Kinkade painting. In Kinkade's words, he paints images that are "warm and welcoming." The reason he paints them, he says, is to "provide comfort and hope" to people.[8] In times of cold comforts and stormy nights, people want warm and cozy. But "huddle and cuddle" can leave you smashed to smithereens on the shoals.

*To live in the present is one of the most difficult challenges we face every day. We keep slipping backward into nostalgia or forward into expectation . . . [We] escape into the sidewaters of remembering or planning.*

SAMUEL HAZO[9]

When Jesus appeared to his frightened disciples on Easter Sunday evening, he did a little show-and-tell. He said "Peace be with you" but then he showed them his hands and his side.[10] The way to peace is not through safety and refuge; Christ's peace comes through risk and vulnerability. The way to peace is not through saving yourself. The way to peace is through laying down your life to save others, not lying low and hunkering down. We're so hunkered down with church-convention legislation, hunkered down with resolutions, hunkered down with programs, hunkered down with buildings: we're so weighed down hunkering that its no wonder we're drowning.

Christians have become like the third servant in Jesus' parable of the talents. He did the safe thing with the single talent he had been given—buried it in the ground, one of the most accepted forms of responsible safekeeping in the first century—but his play-it-safe strategy earned him a place in "the outer darkness" far away from the joy of his master. In taking no risk, he had risked it all. And lost.

Jesus placed himself in the firing line of history. Sometimes he calls us to place ourselves in the firing line of history. "Get out of the boat, Peter." A disciple of Jesus operates within the world of high risk. Lift anchor and head out into the deep waters. Waltz on the bald waves.

*Gently resisting change since 1872*

HIGHWAY BILLBOARD ADVERTISING THE TOWN OF GRUENE, TEXAS[11]

If you want a quiet life, a life of peace and contentment, then don't follow Jesus.

If you want a secure life, a life lived within the margins of safety, then don't follow Jesus.

If you want a life that is all mapped out, a life you can plan and control, then don't follow Jesus.

Faith isn't harbor hugging. Faith is bungee jumping. From an evolutionary perspective, the more risks we take, the more likely we are to survive and thrive. From a faith perspective, life's ultimate risk is not to risk anything. Part of the appeal of the *Forrest Gump* movie was its gentle reminder that playing it safe on the shore during storms can smash you to smithereens, whereas facing storms head on can bring you a fortune.

*With faith I plunge me in this sea,*
*Here is my hope, my joy, my rest; . . .*

*Though waves and storms go o'er my head,*
*Though strength, and health and friends be gone, . . .*

*This anchor shall my soul sustain, . . .*
*Loved with an everlasting love.*

JOHN WESLEY[12]

The church of the perfect storm is a church that is looking and lurching forward, not a church that is stuck in nostalgic, picturesque, or romantic poses. The biggest problem with seminaries today is that they are training ministers to be harbor pilots, when the world needs deep-water captains.[13] Seminaries need to become more like the Weather Channel, providing resources and weather alerts, helping track the storms, and building databases from which to learn. In the words of an

Emily Dickinson poem I memorized my first year of seminary and recited daily as a meditative practice:

> Exultation is the going
> Of an inland soul to sea,
> Past the houses—past the headlands—
> Into deep Eternity—
>
> Bred as we, among the mountains,
> Can the sailor understand
> The divine intoxication
> Of the first league out from land?[14]

*Throw off the bowlines,*
*sail away from the safe harbor,*
*catch the trade winds in your sails.*

ATTRIBUTED TO SAMUEL L. CLEMENS (A.K.A. MARK TWAIN)[15]

## 2. Steer into the Wind

Just as you can't seek shelter and escape the storm, no matter how much we may love to sing the Ira Sankey song "Shelter in the Time of Storm," you can't outrun the storm. Once you're out on the high sea, the worst thing you can do is to try to flee the storm. You can't reverse engines and escape the storm. You can't even batten down the hatches and slip its fury. It will hunt you down and overtake you every time. The turning tides of postmodernity, post-Christendom, and post-scale cannot be turned back or turned off, no matter how *pomo*-phobic you are.

Besides, the gospel of Jesus Christ shows us not how to beat a retreat from the storms plaguing our planet, but how to address and redress the storm fronts that move in. The last stanza of Isaac Watts's 1724 hymn "Am I a Soldier of the Cross?" has a variant version attributed by some to John Newton:

Shall I be wafting to the sky,
On flowery beds of ease.
While others strive to win the prize,
And sail on bloody seas.[16]

Steer into the wind. To turn toward the wind (but never directly *into* the wind) is to turn toward the future, to face and outface the unknown that lies ahead. Once we learn the truth about what is happening in our world, whether we like it or not, we must learn to be at home in the strange times we're in.

This is what bison do and cows do not. When a storm comes on the prairie, buffalo put their heads down and walk into the storm. Cows try to get around the storm, and often get trapped in it. By facing the storm, buffaloes walk out of the storm, while cows get lost and die.[17]

The church has too many cow Christians and not enough buffalo believers.

Jesus walked directly into danger: he set his face toward Jerusalem, never looked back, and steered into the storm. He didn't tell his disciples to run from storms, but to tack into them. He didn't tell his disciples that it's going to be easy. He told his disciples that it's not going to be easy, that it's going to take everything you've got. Maybe only out of spent and broken bodies can a new world rise up?

In the stream of history, do we face the downstream flow, carrying the debris and blunders of the past? Or do we face upstream, poised to rise to the challenge of what might be?[18] To follow Jesus is to follow the future. To follow Jesus is to summon the courage of the future: the courage to lean forward and face the future, a future filled with possibilities, probabilities, and impossibilities. To follow Jesus is not to be pushed from behind into the future; to follow Jesus is to be pulled from in front into the future, where Jesus already is. Jesus is always ahead of us. We are always catching up to him.[19] When Jesus ascended, he ascended as much to the future as to the heavens. In liturgy we remember the future, and the Christ who comes to us from the future ushers us into God's presence. Jesus has already gone ahead of us. To dare to face the wind is to dare to turn and face Jesus, who comes to us from the future.

Christians can be fascinated by the future, but too many don't want to live there. To follow Jesus is to squeeze the long view into the short compass. The next quarter-century may be the most decisive twenty-five-year period in human history. What Winston Churchill liked to say about the individual is even more true of the church: "a man must never allow himself to fall below the level of events." The church must not allow itself to be stranded by history, beached like driftwood, lessened, worn away, or misconceived.

*Launch out into the deep,*
*Oh, let the shore-line go;*
*Launch out, launch out in the ocean divine,*
*Out where the full tides flow.*

A. B. SIMPSON[20]

Two more caveats: first, for aquachurch to follow AquaChrist into the wind, small boats fare better than big supertankers and cruise vessels. When buffeting about in eighty-foot waves, you are better off not having the giant hulls that refuse to give and break under the pounding.

Second, if a storm is severe enough, driving into the wind can become impossible and destroy a ship. The apostle Paul discovered this the hard way when he was headed toward Phoenix, and a storm was so strong the ship found itself with no choice but to let the wind drive it west. Paul survived by not attempting to steer into the wind, but instead letting the wind drive him.

*The ship was caught by the storm and could not head into the wind; so we gave way to it and were driven along.*

ACTS 27:15

There are times when we need to take our hands totally off the controls, and trust the Spirit of God to blow us where it wills. There are times when we need to learn how to be what I call pneumanauts, or sailors of the Spirit.

## 3. Get Rid of Excess Cargo; Toss Heavy Burdens Overboard

*There are concerns which seem indecent when in the company of a cliff.*

ALAIN DE BOTTON[21]

In 1991 the *Andrea Gail* did not survive the Halloween Gale partly because her captain refused to abandon a bulging shipload of swordfish. Two thousand years earlier another October nor'easter[22] seized an Alexandrian ship on which the apostle Paul was traveling, but this time the captain threw the cargo overboard (and even the crew's personal gear),[23] and they survived. Sometimes life requires us to part with those things that are not essential to the mission, excess baggage that may even be causing us to lose the plot of life. The journey of life can pile up big burdens of grudges and grievances which, if not set down, will slow us down if not stop us in our tracks.

Michael Blewett is an Episcopal priest, friend, and contributor to this volume. His seminary mentor at Virginia Theological Seminary, Mark Dyer, taught that about every four hundred years, "the Church needs a yard sale. We are quite overdue for one." All of our tribes need to throw some modern (and even some postmodern) cargo overboard, and simultaneously re-cover, re-new, and re-use some ancient (premodern) treasures we've lost in forgotten corners of the hull.

In fact, the true meaning of *reform* is not innovation, but restoration to origins, to the original condition, to stricter not more liberal observances.[24] Protestant Reformers so understood "reformation." So did the Catholic Reformers of the Second Vatican Council, who adopted a physics of the swing (simultaneously lean back and kick forward) criteria for the "reform" of the church: 1. *ressourcement*, leaning back in a return to the sources, and 2. *aggiornamento*, kicking forward in bringing the church up to date and engaging with culture.

Roots are not always good. Sometimes they can kill a plant, especially if it's trapped in a pot. Like any organic thing, the church can become root-bound, unable to hold water and unable to produce new life. Root-bound structures need to have some of the roots cut away so that new shoots can grow new roots.

One of the strengths of Christianity, and a strength that has enabled Christianity to grow in lots of different soil, is the theological doctrine of *adiaphora* (literally "things indifferent"), which means the freedom to differ in what is not essential, even sometimes the freedom to disagree about what is essential. The guiding yardstick of *adiaphora* is what has kept all reformations from becoming more of a bloodbath than they were. Certain things are indifferent to salvation, even though they may be enormously important to our tribe (are you infralapsarian or supralapsarian? are you TULIP or SERT?). German medieval monk Thomas à Kempis fleshed out the spirit description of an adiaphorist in famous terms: "In things essential, unity; in doubtful things, liberty; in all things, charity."[25] All of faith is not *adiaphora*, but without *adiaphora* (knowing the difference between carryon and cargo, between sandbags that weigh us down and tarp that sails us forth), faith cannot be all in all.

*It's under my feet, when it's over your head.*
*You got nothin' to fear, you got nothin' to dread.*
*Remember my promise and all that I've said,*
*It's under my feet, when it's over your head.*

JOHN WILKIE[26]

Plato liked to compare life to a big triangle. Along the base are those things that we deem important. But the more we move up the triangle to the apex of life, the more we proceed upward, the smaller the base gets and the more we need to get rid of things of lesser importance. For the Christian, there is room at the top of the triangle for only one thing: Jesus Christ.

## 4. Lash Yourself to the Mast of the Master; Steady as She Goes

The more the world spins dizzyingly out of control, the more the need for a fixed point and the more we need to lock our hands on the tiller of truth.

Ancient mariners would sometimes instruct their men to lash them to the helm so that they could pilot the ship through the foulest of winds, the fiercest of waves. In the Ulysses-style lashing, the captain was tied to the mast of the ship, with explicit instructions not to be released, however much one may plead. *Steady as she goes* is the phrase the captain of the ship used to get everyone (including himself) focused, not on staying the course, but on steadying the wheel to better maneuver into the storm. Staying the course, especially courses set before gale-force winds change all cruising lanes, is a decision for death.

The early Christians faced east when they prayed because they believed Jesus would return from that direction. But as time passed, they went from facing east to facing a cross, which became a sort of compass. It is in the cross that we find direction for our lives. Only from the cross can we see ahead.[27]

When others tie themselves hopelessly in knots, tie yourself to the mast of the Master. Christians are found lashed not to pier and pillar, but to the mast of Christ. Let there be no daylight between you and the Master.

When the rest of the world is out of tune, keep striking the middle C of faith, God's tuning fork to the eternal: Jesus the Christ, God's Perfect Pitch, whose vibrations are "the same yesterday, today, and forever." In the midst of the perfect storm, we must lash ourselves to the Word of God; we must strap ourselves to the cross and strike the tuning fork of faith in Christ. You can tell a ship that will make it through the Perfect Storm by the sounding of these words: "I will cling to the old rugged cross." [28]

*Therefore, since we are surrounded by such a great cloud of witnesses, let us throw off everything that hinders [for me—seeking the approval of men] and the sin that so easily entangles [for me—fear, intimidation, unworthiness]. And let us run with perseverance the race marked out for us, fixing our eyes on Jesus, the pioneer and perfecter of faith. For the joy set before him he endured the cross, scorning its shame, and sat down at the right hand of the throne of God. Consider him who endured such opposition from sinners, so that you [and I] will not grow weary and lose heart.*

HEBREWS 12:1-3 TNIV

We are *not* captains of our own ship. And the more we cling to the true Captain, the more we realize that we aren't the ones holding on; Jesus is holding fast to us in the perfecting storms of life. Even if we are afraid, Jesus will embrace us as he did Peter, reaching out his hand and catching him before he sank.[29]

## 5. Enjoy an Epic Ride

It was as if every person present was a live wire, just ripped from its home by the storm, spewing sparks everywhere it touched.

The congregational meeting had been called to respond to the anger that erupted after the Episcopal Church elected its first openly gay bishop. Some members looked around to see who wasn't there (meaning who had already left the church). Others waited anxiously to hear the direction their brothers and sisters were taking.

Toward the end of the meeting, one of the eldest members of the congregation rose to speak. She had been brought to the meeting by her chauffeur and nurse, who also accompanied her each Sunday to the 11 A.M. worship, where she sat smack dab in front of the pulpit, second row. In a firm but feeble voice, she gave her verdict:

> I know a lot of my friends have left this church because of this controversy. And I have listened to some of your decisions tonight, whether to go or to stay. Here is where I am: when you're in a storm, you can ride the wave out and in, or you can ride the wave up and down. This is my church. I'm too old to play the in-and-out game. I'll ride the wave up and down, and enjoy the ride.[30]

Ride the waves, even when the church is in trouble. Lash yourselves to the mast of the cross and the Word of God, making Christ your compass rather than wobbly weather vanes of public opinion. Beware of swimming in the shark-infested waters of bureaucratic suitlands or denominational assemblies.

The devil may be in the scale, but God is in the storm: Jesus has entered the storms of post-scale, postmodern, post-Christendom and has defeated each one of them.

Of all the storm stories in the Bible, my favorite is one that occurred early in Jesus' ministry: the massive storm that swept up the Sea of Galilee into its sudden fury.[31] Blasted by extensive healing work, Jesus instructed his disciples to escape the crowds by getting into the boat and going over to the other side. It doesn't take long for the boat to rock Jesus to sleep. Mark's surprising lushness of details about where Jesus is sleeping (the bow) and what he is sleeping on (a pillow) is the literary equivalent of Jesus having a "Do Not Disturb" sign on his body. Jesus is in a deep sleep and doesn't want to be awakened.

At first the feeling of being swept here and there by the sea is relaxing. But the storm worsens to the point where the boat starts bouncing from side to side. The disciples are now scared and wet to the bone. It takes only one near capsize of the ship for the disciples to look at one another with the same fear in their eyes: "We're gonna die." They had one hope: wake Jesus up. You can be sure they didn't all volunteer for this assignment. No doubt they sent Peter to do the dirty work of waking Jesus up from his exhausted state.

There is no rebuke to the disciples for waking him up, only a rebuke to the sea for disturbing the peace. Jesus walks to the side of the boat and stills the storm.

Let's dress rehearse for our storm by entering into the story from the disciples' point of view. Imagine with me that you are one of the disciples. We have just witnessed one of the greatest miracles of Jesus' ministry, the first time he demonstrated his mastery over nature. Jesus had healed people before this, but there were lots of wandering faith healers in Jesus' day. Here was a healer who could command the wind and the waves to obey him.

If you or I are one of the disciples, I know what we're doing after that miracle: high fiving one another for the wisdom of our choice. Did we pick the right guy to follow, or what? You know so-and-so could never have done what Jesus just did! Are we good or what?

Then we would go from high fiving one another to body-slamming each other, what a blessing. Can you believe that we were the first to be there when Jesus did the impossible? Can you believe what we just saw? Are we blessed or what? We are the first to see Jesus perform the miraculous! What a privilege! What a blessing! We may just have witnessed the greatest miracle in all of recorded history!

And that's exactly what Jesus turns around and says to us, his high fiving, body-slamming disciples. Right? Congratulations, disciples, you've just seen some of my best work?

Wrong.

What Jesus actually says is (to use more academic language): "F."

Jesus often tests his disciples. In fact, the word *tempts*, which appears twenty-one times in the New Testament, means twenty times a test or trial and only once a temptation to sin. And when Jesus tests his disciple, they usually do so well: "Stay Awake;" "Stay in Jerusalem;" and so on.

In a paraphrase of Matthew 8:26, Jesus says in those words "O you of little faith": "Disciples, you failed that test. That's not the real thrill I had in mind for you. You could have ridden history's greatest roller-coaster ride. With me in the boat, and with the Holy Spirit billowing the sails, what do you have to fear? What harm can come to you?" The disciples settled for the lull of their lives rather than the ride of their lives. The church loves to focus on Jesus' first rebuke to the storm, and forgets Jesus' second rebuke to the little-faith disciples.

*The Rock didn't sink:* Jesus is with us, so we can relax and don't have to worry about storms. One comes up. One always comes up. But what is our fear? We can talk to God through our stormy situations. We can ride the waves with peace and joy and pass out kites.

Jesus doesn't promise calm seas. But he does promise to calm us in every sea.

Jesus doesn't promise to speak peace to every storm that comes our way. But he promises to give us perfect peace in the midst of every perfect storm.

The essence of the gospel, in the words of Herbert McCabe, is that if you don't love, you're dead, and if you do, they'll kill you.

As the crew of the *Andrea Gail* found out, there is always one storm bigger than any boat. No one gets out of life alive. Even in this worst case scenario, even if the Rock doesn't walk on water but sinks and drowns, what is the worst that can happen? As long as we are in the boat with Jesus, "[nothing] will be able to separate us from the love of God that is in Christ Jesus our Lord."[32] In fact, "for me, to live is Christ and to die is gain,"[33] and "to be away from the body and at home with the Lord."[34]

When we're in the same boat with Jesus, it all comes out all right in the end.

A long time ago, I read a sermon from some forgotten source where the preacher contrasted two ways of crossing the threshold of those Pearly Gates. When we are swept ashore at the Pearly Gates by that ultimate wave, will Saint Peter be eager to hear us testify about what a harrowing, nightmarish, perilous, troublesome, tempest-tossed thing life has been. "What a heavy cross Jesus gave me to carry, Peter. What a burden it's been."

Or will Saint Peter be more motivated to open those gates by hearing us say, "Wow, Peter, what a ride!"

Might not the first question at Judgment Day be, "did you *enjoy* your life, my creation?"

When trust in God "knows the despairs of the world," when trust in

God leads us through the perfect storm, "we began to conceive hopes greater than all our fears," as John Newton would put it.[35] Or in the *best* lines of any Christmas carol:

> The hopes and fears of all the years
> Are met in thee [. . .] tonight.[36]

They aren't met in Jerusalem or Washington. They aren't met in Fort Knox or Las Vegas, Beijing or Bangkok. The "hopes and fears of all the years" are met in a little town of Bethlehem, where an ancient-mariner baby born in a manger made all the difference in this storm-tossed world.

*I will not die an unlived life.*
*I will not live in fear*
*of falling or catching fire.*
*I choose to inhabit my days,*
*to allow my living to open me,*
*to make me less afraid,*
*more accessible,*
*to loosen my heart*
*until it becomes a wing,*
*a torch, a promise.*
*I choose to risk my significance,*
*to live so that which came to me as seed*
*goes to the next as blossom,*
*and that which came to me as blossom,*
*goes on as fruit.*

DAWNA MARKOVA[37]

# LIST OF CONTRIBUTORS

Thomas G. Bandy: www.easumbandy.com. Tom is president of Easum, Bandy and Associates and executive director of *Net Results* magazine (www.netresults.org). He consults with churches and coaches church leaders in North America and internationally across the spectrum of denominations and cultures. He is the author of numerous books in church growth, mission leadership, and faith formation, and frequent lecturer and seminar leader.

Mark Batterson: www.theaterchurch.com, www.markbatterson.com. Mark serves as lead pastor of National Community Church (NCC) in Washington DC. NCC was recognized as one of the Twenty-five Most Innovative Churches in America in 2007 by *Outreach* magazine. Focused on reaching emerging generations, NCC also owns and operates the largest coffeehouse on Capitol Hill, Ebenezers, recognized in 2007 as the number two coffeehouse in the metro DC area by *AOL CityGuide*. He is the author of two books: *ID: The True You* and *In a Pit with a Lion on a Snowy Day*. And he blogs at www.markbatterson.com. Mark is married to Lora. They live on Capitol Hill with their three children: Parker, Summer, and Josiah.

Michael Blewett: www.csmsg.org. Michael is an Episcopal priest at the Church of Saint Michael and Saint George (Saint Louis, Missouri).

He is the husband of Heather Blewett, also an Episcopal priest, the father of two boys, a teacher, speaker, and author of the blog "Under God's Fingernails."

Bill Easum: www.easumbandy.com. Bill is cofounder of Easum, Bandy and Associates, a church consulting group dedicated to guiding Christian leaders for ancient mission in the contemporary world. Bill is the author of more than a dozen books including *Dancing With Dinosaurs*, *Sacred Cows Make Gourmet Burgers*, *Unfreezing Moves*, *Leadership on the Other Side*, *Go Big*, and *A Second Resurrection.*

Greg Glatz: myspace.com/gregglatz. Greg has been the lead pastor of Central Baptist Church in Winnipeg, Manitoba, since 1993. He is the lead guitar player for the Royal Unruh Band and a doctoral student at George Fox University. Greg is currently cohosting the *GodTalk* radio program on CJOB/68, Manitoba's information super station. He is also developing new approaches to leadership development and spiritual formation through internet technologies.

Alan Jamieson: prodigal.typepad.com. Alan is a senior pastor and sociologist. He leads the pastoral team at the Central Baptist Church in the city center of New Zealand's capital of Wellington. His internationally acclaimed first book, *A Churchless Faith*, drew on his Ph.D. research on why people leave churches and what happens to their Christian faith after leaving.  Subsequent publications include *Journeying in Faith* (2004), *Church Leavers* (2006), and *Chrysalis* (2007).

Stephan Joubert: www.echurch.co.za. Stephan teaches at the University of Pretoria as extraordinary professor in theology. He also writes a daily column for a large South African newspaper, hosts a weekly radio program on national radio, and is the editor of an Afrikaans cyberchurch with about forty thousand members. Stephan has translated the Bible into modern-day Afrikaans and published thirty something academic and Christian books. He lives with his wife and two daughters in Johannesburg, South Africa.

Younglae Kim: www.epictivity.com. Younglae is a scholar, preacher, educator, and global connector. He is a board member of SpiritVenture Ministries and heads up SpiritVenture Ministries Korea. He has received graduate degrees from Drew (M.Div), Yale (S.T.M), and Columbia (Ph.D). Currently he is professor of Christian education at Methodist Theological Seminary, Seoul, Korea. He has translated several of Leonard Sweet's books into Korean and is writing books and doing public lectures on Future Church and Education.

Dries Lombaard: www.echurch.co.za. Dries is currently serving as director of equipping and training in the Dutch Reformed Church Moreleta Park in Pretoria, South Africa (a megachurch with around fifteen thousand members). He is also a regular contributor to the e-church and is active as a leadership consultant and coach in the African church environment. Dries is heavily involved in various interdenominational ventures and initiatives, regularly facilitates leadership tours abroad, and coordinates visits from leading thinkers, futurists and practitioners to Southern Africa. Dries is married to Rethea, and the proud father of three daughters.

Earl J. Pierce: www.stjohnbhc.org. Earl currently serves as pastor of Saint John Evangelical Lutheran Church of the Valley in Bullhead City, Arizona. Before this he was the mission and stewardship executive for Iowa District West of the Lutheran Church-Missouri Synod. In this role he developed a number of resources for congregational revitalization that are in use nationwide. Pierce believes that we must be like the "men of Issachar, who understood the times and knew what Israel should do" (1 Chr 12:32 NIV) in order to sail through the perfect storm.

Leonard Sweet: www.leonardsweet.com, www.sermons.com, and *The Eleven* (2008). Len is currently the E. Stanley Jones Professor of Evangelism at Drew Theological School (Madison, New Jersey), and Visiting Distinguished Professor at George Fox University (Portland, Oregon). He is the author of more than one hundred articles, six hundred published sermons, and thirty books, most recently *The Gospel According to Starbucks* (2007). In both 2006 and 2007, he was voted "One of the Fifty Most Influential Christians in America" (www.thechurchreport.com). His weekly free podcast is called "Napkin Scribbles," and a longer subscription-based weekly podcast is available from WiredParish.com. He lives in the San Juan Islands.

Peter J. Walker: www.theooze.org. A divinity student at George Fox Seminary, Peter is a featured writer in Spencer Burke's "Out of the OOZE" and a charter contributor to Len Sweet's "wikiletics." Peter is dedicated to redreaming the Christianity of his childhood and discovering something fresh, transcendent, effervescent, and emerging by any means necessary. He is convinced that the Holy Spirit is working in places we rarely expect (like taverns, gay bars, and sometimes even churches!). He lives in Oregon with his wife and their agnostic cat.

## Acknowledgments

1. William Cowper, "God Moves in a Mysterious Way," *The Methodist Hymnal: Official Hymnal of the Methodist Church* (Baltimore: The Methodist Publishing House, 1939), 68.

## Introduction: Born in a Storm

1. Scarface, "Sorry 4 What," *Last of a Dying Breed* (Virgin Records, 2000).

2. So argues Colin Buchanan, former bishop Suffragan of Woolwich, and on the Advisory Board of *The Oxford Guide to the Book of Common Prayer: A Worldwide Survey* (New York: Oxford University Press, 2007).

3. Jeremiah 12: 5 TNIV.

4. John 16:33 NKJV.

5. Psalm 4:7 NKJV. Another translation puts it like this: "You have given my heart more joy than they have when grain and wine abound," Psalm 4:8 NAB. Or "You have put into my heart a greater happiness than others had from grain and wine in plenty," Psalm 4:7 REB.

6. William Cowper, "God Moves in a Mysterious Way," *The Methodist Hymnal: Official Hymnal of the Methodist Church* (Baltimore: The Methodist Publishing House, 1939), 68.

## 1. Outstorming Christianity's Perfect Storm

1. Rascal Flatts, "Mayberry," *Melt* (Lyric Street Records, 2002).

2. Tim McGraw, "Back When," *Live Like You Were Dying* (Curb Records, 2004).

3. See Jeff Zaleski, "Focus," the editor's introduction to the "Home" issue of *Parabola* 31 (Winter 2006): 5.

4. I borrow this metaphor from Sebastian Junger's *The Perfect Storm: A True Story of Men Against the Sea* (New York: Norton, 1997), which analyzes the most powerful

North Atlantic storm of the twentieth century: the Halloween Gale of October 27–31, 1991. Junger's story focuses on one swordfishing ship based in Gloucester, Massachusetts, the *Andrea Gail*, that sank in that storm and was never heard from again. That storm resulted from the convergence of three forces: Hurricane Grace coming from the south, a cold front from the north, and a classic nor'easter—the bane of Grand Banks fishermen—that blew in from the Great Lakes region. As these three storms combined over Sable Island, they created a storm so severe it ripped many New England houses off their foundations and took them out to sea.

5. The exact quote is "Yet human beings are born to trouble as surely as sparks fly upward" (Job 5:7 TNIV).

6. As relayed in Charles Curran, "From Division to Unity," *The Tablet* 15 (April 2006); 22-23.

7. See, for example, P. J. Walsh, *Augustine: De Civitate Dei, Books I & II*, ed. and trans. P. J. Walsh (Oxford: Oxbow Books, 2005), 5: "The world is and will remain an arena of violence and injustice, but we are not to retire from it; we must seek to implant justice in it, but the difficulties of establishing peace and justice are enormous." For more see David Lyon, *Postmodernity* (Minneapolis: University of Minnesota Press, 1994), 84.

8. Abraham Lincoln, "Annual Message to Congress," (December 1, 1862) in *The Collected Works of Abraham Lincoln*, vol. 5, ed. Roy P. Basler (New Brunswick, N.J.: Rutgers University Press, 1953), 537.

9. For another metaphor of converging catastrophes, see James Howard Kustler, *The Long Emergency: Surviving the Converging Catastrophes of the Twenty-first Century* (New York: Atlantic Monthly Press, 2005).

10. This was the subject of my book of almost a decade ago *Soul Tsunami: Sink or Swim in a New Millennium Culture* (Grand Rapids, Mich.: Zondervan, 1999). Since then the literature on this tsunami of postmodernity has been voluminous and noisy. See the writings of Reggie McNeal, Rex Miller, Brian McLaren, Thomas Hohstadt, Mark Pierson, Alan Hirsch, or Joe Myers.

11. For those who argue it is, see George Barna, *Revolution* (Wheaton, Ill.: Tyndale House, 2005); Shane Claiborne, *Irresistible Revolution: Living as an Ordinary Radical* (Grand Rapids, Mich.: Zondervan, 2006); Brian McLaren, *A New Kind of Christian: A Tale of Two Friends on a Spiritual Journey* (San Francisco: Jossey-Bass, 2001) and *The Story We Find Ourselves In: Further Adventures of a New Kind of Christian* (San Francisco: Jossey-Bass, 2003).

12. As quoted in *Independent Sector*, "In Memoriam: Writings of John W. Gardner: . . . Additional Writings." http://www.independentsector.org/about/gardner_writings.html (accessed February 3, 2006).

13. Søren Kierkegaard, *Kierkegaard's Concluding Unscientific Postscript*, trans. David F. Swenson and Walter Lowrie (Princeton, N.J.: Princeton University Press, 1941), 182: "If I wish to preserve myself in faith I must constantly be intent upon holding fast the objective uncertainty, so as to remain out upon the deep, over seventy thousand fathoms of water, still preserving my faith."

14. Luke 14:25-33.

15. Or what Augustine called in a marvelous wordplay "*mare malum, mare amarum*" ("the evil sea, the bitter sea"), as quoted in Peter Dronke, *Imagination in the Late Pagan and Early Christian World: The First Nine Centuries A.D.* (Florence, Italy: SISMEL, Edizioni del Galluzzo, 2003), 75.

16. See Hebrews 12:26-27 TNIV: "At that time his voice shook the earth, but now he has promised, 'Once more I will shake not only the earth but also the heavens.' The words 'once more' indicate the removing of what can be shaken—that is, created things—so that what cannot be shaken may remain." Thanks to Stephen Ozment for reminding me of this verse.

17. Colin Morris, *Things Shaken—Things Unshaken: Reflections on Faith and Terror* (London: Epworth Press, 2006), 156.

18. Samuel Johnson, *The Rambler*, no. 2, Saturday March 24, 1750, in *Harrison's British Classics, vol. 1, Containing Dr. Johnson's* Rambler, *and Lord Lyttelton's Persian Letters* (London; Printed for Harrison and Co., 1785), 6.

19. Quote by John Bell © WGRG, Iona Community, G2 3Dh, Scotland. Used by permission (10 August 2007, Victoria@iona.org.uk). Duncan B. Forrester uses this poem to end his book *Apocalypse Now: Reflections on Faith in a Time of Terror* (Burlington, Vt.: Ashgate, 2005), 174-75.

20. This is, of course, a play on Oscar Hamerstein's "Oh What a Beautiful Mornin'" from *Oklahoma* (1943).

21. See "It's No Game," *Economist* 11 (February 2006): 42. See also "PhilSports Arena Stampede," from *Wikipedia*, the Free Encyclopedia, http://en.wikipedia.org/wiki/PhilSports_Arena_stampede (accessed March 16, 2006).

22. Quoted in Haddon Robinson, "Listening to the Listeners," *Leadership: A Journal for Church Leaders* 4 (Spring 1983): 69.

23. For the story and the speech, see "Speech at Peoria, Illinois, October 16, 1854," *The Collected Works of Abraham Lincoln*, vol. 2, 247-83.

24. Stanley J. Grenz, *A Primer on Postmodernism* (Grand Rapids, Mich.: William B. Eerdmans,1996), 12.

25. Daniel J. Adams, "Toward a Theological Understanding of Postmodernism," *Cross Currents* 47 (Winter 1997-98): 520.www.crosscurrents.org/adams.htm (accessed September 11, 2006).

26. James Romaine, "The Visual Arts: The Future Waits Quietly Amidst the Present," in "Redeeming the Time: A Symposium," *Image: A Journal of the Arts and Religion* 42 (Spring/Summer 2004): 33.

27. Jimmy Long, *Generating Hope: A Strategy for Reaching the Postmodern Generation* (Downers Grove, Ill.: InterVarsity Press, 1997), 61.

28. The premodern sense of the self is almost inconceivable today: "in Greek or Roman times, most of us would not have been considered persons, not just in this exalted, tragic sense but even in the barest legal meaning. In Roman law, only the father of a family , the *paterfamilias*, was a person in the eyes of the law; all the members of his household, including his children and slaves, fell under his authority, which gave him absolute right over their lives, including the right to kill them at will. Not to mention the subjection of his slaves or wife or daughters, even his sons did not become persons

while the father lived, no matter how old they were, unless their father specifically gave them their personhood. In order to give public form to this ceremony of manumission, early Roman jurists evolved a kind of legal pantomime whose gestures could be read by the illiterate. The father ceremonially slapped his son with a gentle blow on the cheek, turning him around to face the court as a person. This legal theater of a violent encounter between father and sons reminds one of the tragic drama that seemed to the Greeks the crucible of personhood. Following this confrontation, the son metaphorically puts on the persona by which the court recognizes him as a being of sufficient independent power that he may be heard in legal deliberations." Peter Pesic, *Seeing Double: Shared Identities in Physics, Philosophy, and Literature* (Cambridge, Mass.: MIT Press, 2003), 53.

29. Modern more male, postmodern more female . . . one author even changes the pronoun when he talks of modern ("he") and postmodern ("she"). For his explanation, see Heath White, *Postmodernism 101: A First Course for the Curious Christian* (Grand Rapids, Mich.: Brazos Press, 2006), 20.

30. "The climactic fulfilment of modernity's essential aim: replacing God with Me." Thomas de Zengotita, *Mediated: How The Media Shapes Your World and The Way You Live In It* (New York: Bloomsbury, 2005), 266.

31. Christianity's apocalyptic inheritance claimed that faith is contrary to what is "reasonable"—love your enemy; paradox!

32. How did the church handle modernity's newly created sovereign state ("nation state")? The church flattered them with spiritual flummery, giving rise to civil religion.

33. Tertullian, *Apologeticus* 28. Quoted in Duncan B. Forrester, *Apocalypse Now: Reflections on Faith in a Time of Terror* (Burlington, Vt.: Ashgate, 2005), 19.

34. David Hume, *A Treatice of Human Nature*, ed. L. A. Selby-Bigge; 2nd ed. rev. P. H. Nidditch (New York: Oxford University Press, 1978), 269, 270. Quoted in Peter Pesic, *Seeing Double: Shared Identities in Physics, Philosophy, and Literature* (Cambridge, Mass.: MIT Press, 2003), 38.

35. Reinhold Niebuhr, *An Interpretation of Christian Ethics* (New York: Harper & Brothers, 1935), 3.

36. Heath White, *Postmodernism 101: A First Course for the Curious Christian* (Grand Rapids, Mich.: Brazos Press, 2006), 49.

37. "Reason . . . is not the universal solution that modernism thought it was. The upshot is that resolving basic questions is not a matter of having the right knowledge. Finding answers to these questions is, at minimum, not a matter of finding the truth." Heath White's *Postmodernism 101: A First Course for the Curious Christian* (Grand Rapids, Mich.: Brazos Press, 2006), 46.

38. Zygmunt Bauman, *Modernity and the Holocaust* (Ithaca, N.Y.: Cornell University Press, 1989), x: "The Holocaust was born and executed in our modern rational society, at the high stage of our civilization and at the peak of human cultural achievement."

39. The actual Benjamin Franklin quote is this: "So convenient a thing it is to be a reasonable Creature, since it enables one to find or make a Reason for everything one has a mind to do." Benjamin Franklin, *The Autobiography and Other Writings on Politics,*

*Economics, and Virtue*, ed. Alan Houston (New York: Cambridge University Press, 2004), 29.

40. Richard Rorty, as quoted in Edith Hall, "Would I Lie to You," *Times* (London) (May 28, 2005), http://www.timesonline.co.uk/article/0,,923-1628969,00.html (accessed February 8, 2006).

41. Isa 59:14-15 TNIV.

42. Richard Rohr, *Everything Belongs: The Gift of Contemplative Prayer* (New York: Crossway Books, 1999), 56.

43. Jerry Fodor, "On that Bumpy Road," *TLS: Times Literary Supplement*, 30 (September 2005): 3.

44. Jean Baudrillard, *Simulacra and Simulation*, trans. Sheila Faria Glaser (Ann Arbor, Mich.: The University of Michigan Press, 1994), 1.

45. I use these metaphors in *Soul Tsunami: Sink or Swim in New Millennium Culture* (Grand Rapids, Mich.: Zondervan Publishing House, 1999); in *AquaChurch* (Loveland, Colo.: Group, 1999); from terra firma to aqua; now in *The Church of the Perfect Storm*. I'm not the only one: sociologists David Lyon (he's mentioned in chapter 1 of *Liquid Church*) and Zygmunt Bauman have also used them (Zygmunt Bauman, *Liquid Modernity* [Malden, Mass.: Blackwell, 2000]); as has Pete Ward in *Liquid Church* (Peabody, Mass.: Hendrickson, 2002).

> Bauman explains the extent of the change [from modern to postmodern] by contrasting fluids that 'travel easily . . . flow, spill, run out, splash, pour, leak, flood, spray, drip, seep and ooze' with solids which are fixed, dependable and stable. He argues that the solids of modernity are being liquefied not so they can be reformed into new solid structures but to remain perpetually in fluid motion under the new conditions of postmodernity. As this happens there is a loss of the old foundations: a loss of order, of structures and of systems. Living in this emerging 'liquid' world is metaphorically like leaving the dry land to travel at sea. In this liquid world the church is one of the structures—a solid—that is being liquefied.

See Alan Jamieson, *Journeying in Faith: In and Beyond The Tough Places* (London: SPCK, 2004), 146.

46. Kevin Wilson, "Christian Beliefs Aren't a Threat," Letters to the Editor, *USA Today*, 09 June 2006, 15A. http://www.usatoday.com/news/opinion/editorials/2006-06-08-letters-other_x.htm (accessed June 29, 2006).

47. Martin Robinson & Dwight Smith, *Invading Secular Space: Strategies for Tomorrow's Church* (Grand Rapids, Mich.: Monarch Books, 2003), 204, report that "the number of churches in India has grown from 150,000 20 years ago to some 400,000 today."

48. "Post-Christendom includes the following transitions: From the centre to margins. . . . From majority to minority. . . . From settlers to sojourners. . . . From privilege to plurality. . . . From control to witness. . . . From maintenance to mission. . . . From institution to movement." Stuart Murray, *Post-Christendom* (Waynesboro, Ga.: Paternoster, 2004), 20.

49. In his theological autobiography, Douglas John Hall writes: "the question confronting serious Christians in the west today is whether the Christian faith is able to address a civilization no longer on the rise, but falling, visibly in decline—and tempted in

its decline, as ancient Rome was, to seek its continued glory and power in ever more aggressive and bellicose acts, designed by leaders who do no "do nuance."' Douglas John Hall, *Bound and Free: A Theologian's Journey* (Minneapolis: Fortress Press, 2005), 71.

50. See also the writings of Douglas John Hall, who stresses the end of Christendom: "The Rise and Fall of Christendom," *Sewanee Theological Review* 36 (1993): 463-71; *The End of Christendom and the Future of Christianity* (Eugene, Ore.: Wipf & Stock, 1997, 2002); "Discipleship in a Post-Christendom Context: Contemplating the Proclamation of the Gospel for the Salvation of Humankind," *Church & Society* 88 (July-August 1998):93-105; "Metamorphosis: From Christendom to Diaspora," *Confident Witness–Changing World* (Grand Rapids, Mich.: Eerdmans 1999), 67-79; "Confessing Christ in a Post-Christendom Context," *Ecumenical Review* 52 (July 2000): 410-17; "On Being a Church After Christendom," *In Essentials Unity: Reflections on the Nature and Purpose of the Church: in Honor of Frederick R. Trost*, ed. M. Douglas Meeks and Robert D. Mutton (Minneapolis: Kirk House, 2001), 43-49.

51. Quoted in Leonard I. Sweet's review of *Morality and the Mail in 19th Century America*, by Wayne E. Fuller, Journal of American History 91 (September 2004): 626. Emerson's actual quote is "The name of Jesus is not so much written as plowed into the history of the world." As quoted in Herschal Hobbs, *The Life and Times of Jesus: A Contemporary Approach* (Grand Rapids, Mich.: Zondervan, 1966), 7.

52. W. H. Auden, "The History of Truth," *Collected Poems* (London: Faber and Faber, 1976), 463. The second line is: "Truth was the most of many credibles."

53. Nazi diatribe from a newspaper article, Pomerania, Germany, mid-1930s and quoted by Art Spiegelman, *Maus: A Survivor's Tale, II: And Here My Troubles Begin* (New York: Pantheon, 1991), 4.

54. Callum Brown, *The Death of Christian Britain: Understanding Secularism, 1800–2000* (New York: Routledge, 2001), 1.

55. As quoted in Ruth Gledhill, "Bishop Warns Church that It May Disappear," *Times* (London), March 20, 2004, Timesonline, http://www.timesonline.co.uk/article/0,,2-1044655,00.html. Published in the Foreword to *The UK Christian Handbook: Religious Trends* (London: Christian Research, 2004)

56. Stuart Murray, *Post-Christendom* (Waynesboro, Ga.: Paternoster Press, 2005), 1.

57. Edward Knippers, "The Old, Old Story" in *It Was Good Making Art to the Glory of God*, ed. Ned Bustard (Baltimore, MD: Square Halo Books, 2000), 94.

58. Nicholas Lash, *Holiness, Speech and Silence: Reflections on the Question of God* (Ashgate, 2004), 2-3.

59. Theo Hobson, "Holistic Spirit: *The Tablet* Interview with Linda Woodhead," *The Tablet* (June 10, 2006): 6, http://www.thetablet.co.uk/cgi-bin/archive_db.cgi/tablet-01202 (accessed June 28, 2006).

60. I got this image from a personal conversation with Dan Kimball, author of *The Emerging Church: Vintage Christianity for New Generations* (Grand Rapids, Mich.: Zondervan, 2003).

61. Murray, *Post-Christendom*, 1.

62. See Philip Pullman, *His Dark Materials Trilogy* (New York: Alfred A. Knopf,

1996-2000): *The Golden Compass* (1996), *The Subtle Knife* (1997), *The Amber Spy Glass* (2000).

63. With thanks to Michael Irwin of Cranleigh, Surrey, for these quotes. See Richard Dawkins, *The God Delusion* (Boston: Houghton Mifflin, 2006) 43.

64. White, *Postmodernism 101: A First Course for the Curious Christian*, 63.

65. Denis Diderot, as quoted in *The Oxford Dictionary of Political Quotations*, 2nd ed., ed. Antony Jay (New York: Oxford University Press, 2001), 110.

66. Virginia Woolf, "To Vanessa Bell, 11 February 1928," in *The Letters of Virginia Woolf, ed. Nigel Nicolson and Joanne Trautmann* (New York: Harcourt, Brace Jovanovich, 1977), 3, 457-58.

67. John Haffenden, *William Empson: Among the Mandarins* (New York: Oxford University Press 2005), 62-65. See also William Empson, *Milton's God*, rev. ed. (London: Chatto & Windus, 1965), where his contempt of Christianity (followed closely by Communism) is most clearly shown. Here is one example: "I have thus to conclude that the doctrine of the Trinity is a means of deceiving good men into accepting evil; it is the double-talk by which Christians hide from themselves the insane wickedness of their God" (245).

68. Gore Vidal, "Sex Is Politics," *Gore Vidal: Sexually Speaking: Collected Sex Writings*," ed. Donald Weise (San Francisco: Cleis Press, 1999), 100. The essay was originally published in *Playboy*, January 1979.

69. Noel Annan, *The Dons: Mentors, Eccentrics and Geniuses* (Chicago: University of Chicago Press, 1999), 3: "I failed to persuade Francis to allow his name to go forward for a fellowship at King's. He would not join any society with a chapel: to do so would have been to connive at error; and King's undeniably had a chapel."

70. See the November 2006 cover headline "The New Atheism: No Heaven, No Hell, Just Science: Inside the Crusade Against Religion" and the interview with Richard Dawkins, Sam Harris, and Daniel Dennett by Gary Wolf, "The Church of the Non-Believers," *Wired* 11 (November 2006), 182-93, www.wired.com/wired/archive/14.11/atheism.html (accessed December 20, 2006).

71. Dawkins's popularity stems in part from his borrowing of Richard Semon's concept of the meme in the early twentieth century and making the language of "memes" famous: "memes are mental constructs that propagate through minds, much as genes do through bodies." See Tim Flannery, "Howling Monkeys," *TLS: Times Literary Supplement*, 19 November 2004, 3-4.

72. Of course, Dawkins is as every much a fundamentalist as those he opposes: he's an Enlightenist fundamentalist, or a scientific fundamentalist.

73. As quoted by John Morrish, "Dawkins on Crusade," *The Tablet*, 14 January 2006, 27. See also Keith Ward, "Faith, Hype and a Lack of Clarity," *The Tablet*, 21 January 2006, 4-5.

74. Channel 4—Can You Believe It? Debates and Controversies—"The Root of All Evil?" http://www.channel4.com/culture/microsites/C/can_you_believe_it/debates/rootofevil1.html (accessed July 7, 2006). Stephen Weinberg's quote is from his "A Designer Universe," based on a talk given in April 1999 at the Conference on Cosmic Design of the American Association for the Advancement of Science,

Washington DC. http://www.physlink.com/Education/essay_weinberg.cfm (accessed July 7, 2006).

75. The best critique of Dawkins's book is Terry Eagleton's "Lunging, Flailing, Mispunching," *London Review of Books*, 19 October 2006, 32-34. One example will suffice: "On the horrors that science and technology have wreaked on humanity, [Dawkins] is predictably silent. Yet the Apocalypse is far more likely to be the product of them than the work of religion. Swap you the inquisition for chemical warfare" (34).

76. See Daniel Clement Dennett, *Breaking the Spell: Religion as a Natural Phenomenon* (New York: Viking, 2006), 51. The critique of intelligent design by both these scientists is very similar. In fact, Dawkins borrows Dennett's language that the cosmic Designer is portrayed as a "skyhook," a "supernatural pseudo-solution that merely postpones the question of where the designer came from. What is needed instead of the skyhook is a 'crane'—a mechanism that can yield complex phenomena from very simple basic principles." Quote is from John Cottingham, "Flawed Case for Prosecution," review of Richard Dawkins, *The God Delusion*, *The Tablet* (October 19, 2006): 22, http://www.thetablet.co.uk/reviews/312 (accessed June 28, 2007).

77. Sam Harris, *The End of Faith: Religion, Terror, and the Future of Reason* (New York: W. W. Norton & Co., 2004), 52-53.

78. Frederick Crews, "The New Creationists and Their Friends," in his *Follies of the Wise: Dissenting Essays* (Emeryville, Calif.: Shoemaker Hoard, 2006), 264.

79. Jerry A. Coyne, "Cause and Reason," review of Daniel C. Dennett, *Breaking the Spell: Religion as a Natural Phenomenon* (London: Allen Lane, 2006), *TLS: Times Literary Supplement*, (March 31, 2006): 24.

80. Alan Hirsch, *The Forgotten Ways* (Grand Rapids, Mich.: Brazos Books, 2007), 65.

81. Theodore Dalrymple, *Our Culture, What's Left of It: The Mandarins and the Masses* (Chicago: Dee, 2006), 53.

82. STEM is an acronym for Science, Technology, Engineering, and Mathematics.

83. See "The World Has a Lot of Problems," *Business 2.0* (January/February 2007): 22-23. The statistics cited for each of these problems are as follows. 1. Greenhouse Gases: "The average American's use of transportation and electricity releases 10 tons of carbon dioxide into the atmosphere each year. The goods and services she consumes are responsible for 14 tons more. That leads to . . ." 2. Global Warming: "By 2050 the melting of Greenland's land-based ice cap into the Atlantic will raise the sea level worldwide by 23 feet—and put [Boston, Atlantic City, Norfolk, Jacksonville, New Orleans, Miami, and Galveston] at risk." 3. Dying Oceans: "By 2048 all species of commercially caught fish could decline to less than 10 percent of 1950 levels." 4. Famine: "Every minute 12 children worldwide die of hunger."5. Superbugs: "Just 25 years ago, roughly 3 percent of the common but deadly staph bacteria were resistant to antibiotics. Today almost 60 percent are." 6. Trash: "China generated 784 million tons of industrial waste in 1999. In 2005 that number was 1.3 billion tons." 7. Unclean Water: "One out of five people lacks access to uncontaminated drinking water. 8. Epidemics: "There are 300 million cases of malaria annually—90 percent of them in Africa." 9. Air Pollution: "South Asia is covered with a two-mile-thick toxic cloud that kills 500,000 people a year in India alone."

84. Ronald Wright, *A Short History of Progress* (New York: Carroll & Graf, 2005), 7.

85. Ibid., 8.

86. Ibid.

87. In his book *Apocalypse Now? Reflections on Faith in a Time of Terror* (Burlington, Vt.: Ashgate, 2005), 50, Duncan Forrester quotes Henry Wieman's exaggerated declaration that "The bomb that fell on Hiroshima cut history in two like a knife . . . That cut is more abrupt, decisive and revolutionary than the cut made by the star over Bethlehem."

88. Wright, *A Short History of Progress*, 7.

89. Ibid., 107.

90. Martin J. Rees, *Our Final Hour: A Scientist's Warning: How Terror, Error, and Environmental Disaster Threaten Humankind's Future in This Century* (New York: Basic Books, 2003), 74.

91. As quoted in Justin Fox and David Kirkpatrick, "Brainstorm 2003:To Hell in a Handbasket . . . or to Heaven via High Tech? Deep Thinkers Debate the State of the World at *Fortune*'s Aspen Conference," *Fortune* (October 27, 2003): 176, http://www.fortune.com/fortune/subs/columnist/0,15704,517343,00.html (accessed January 25, 2005).

92. Alyssa Ford, "Humanity: The Remix: Is Building a Better Human the Key to Utopia or the World's Most Dangerous Idea?" *Utne*, (May–June 2005): 54. http://www.utne.com/cgi-bin/udt/im.display.printable?client.id=utne&story.id=11638 (accessed February 21, 2006).

93. Atwood is a phrasemaker par excellence. This is her description of cat's eyes: "clear glass with a bloom of colored petals in the center . . . the eyes of something that isn't known but exists anyway." Margaret Atwood, *Cat's Eye* (New York: Doubleday, 1989), 66, 67. She is referring to marbles not cats! (67).

94. For more on Atwood's signature LongPen, see http://www.technovelgy.com/ct/Science-Fiction-News.asp?NewsNum=556. See also http://www.theage.com.au/articles/2006/03/06/1141493568372.html; you can find the Unotchit, LongPen website at http://www.unotchit.com/ (accessed May 6, 2006). Also see Steven, Zeitchik, "Book Biz Gets Helping Hand. (Smoke & Mirrors: Behind the Scenes of the Biz's Deals, Decisions and Diversions) (LongPen, robotic arm that enable signing authographs remotely), *Variety* 402 (March 6, 2006): 4; "With LongPen, Author Signs Books from Afar," *The Age* (March 6, 2006), http://www.theage.com.au/news/breaking/longpen-makes-its-debut/2006/03/06/1141493568372.html (accessed May 1, 2006). Also Oliver Burkeman, "Red Faces as Revolutionary Pen Draws a Blank, *The Age* (March 7, 2006), http://www.theage.com.au/articles/2006/03/06/1141493690887.html (accessed May 6, 2006); Leigh Anne Williams, "Dear Fan: It Was Very Nice to Not Meet You," *Time Canada* (March 20, 2006): 6; Jill Lawless, "Margaret Atwood Unveils the LongPen, High-tech Tool for Tired Authors," *Seattle Times* (March 6, 2006), http://archives.seattletimes.nwsource.com/cgibin/texis/web/vortex/display?slug=atwood06&date=20060306.

95. Richard Louv, *Last Child in The Woods: Saving Our Children from Nature-Deficit Disorder* (Chapel Hill, N.C.: Algonquin Books of Chapel Hill, 2005), 10.

96. The GRIN acronym comes from of Joel Garreau, *Radical Evolution: The Promise and Peril of Enhancing Our Minds, Our Bodies–and What It Means to Be Human* (New York: Doubleday, 2005), 4-5.

97. Quoted by Van Wishard, "Understanding Our Moment in History: Living Between Two Ages," *Vital Speeches of the Day* 71 (May 1, 2005), 445. Also as a presentation to the Kendal Forum, Kennett Square, Pa., *World Trend Research*, http://www.worldtrendsresearch.com/books/understanding-moment-history.html (accessed May 9, 2006).

98. A term first used by Brent Schlender, "The Edison of the Internet," *Fortune* (February 15, 1999): 84-90, http://www.fortune.com/fortune/subs/article/0,15114,376666,00.html (accessed January 25, 2005). For Joy's concern see "The Other Bill," *Economist* (September 21, 2002): 29-30.

99. For more on the promises and perils of GRIN progress, see Bill Joy, "Why the Future Doesn't Need Us," *Wired* 8 (April 2000), 238-40. Bill Joy is not the first scientist to reflect on how his work affects the entire social order. Decades earlier (1974) came the "Berg" letter (it led to the Asilomar conference on recombinant DNA research in 1975), which called attention to the potential dangers of GNR research and asked for a moratorium. Nobel laureate Paul Berg signed it, as did Jim Watson, Ron Davis, Dave Hogness, Stan Cohen, and other eminent biologists. The letter urged their colleagues to cease and desist certain experiments using "artificial recombinant DNA molecules" because of their unknown consequences. It called for a voluntary moratorium on certain types of recombinant DNA experiments until the hazards could be assessed. See "Potential Biohazards of Recombinant DNA Molecules," letter signed by the Committee on Recombinant DNA Molecules Assembly of Life Sciences, National Research Council, National Academy of Sciences, Washington, DC, *Science* (July 26, 1974): 303. See also Nicholas Wade, "Genetic Manipulation: Temporary Embargo Proposed on Research," *Science* (July 26, 1974): 332-34. For further information see Paul Berg, "Asilomar and Recombinant DNA." Nobelprize.org, http://nobelprize.org/chemistry/articles/berg/index.html (accessed June 1, 2006).

100. Many are arguing that genetics is the number one industry of the future. Almost certain will GRIN collectively be the top industry of the future.

101. Nanotechnology is "bottom-up" technology—the manipulation of atom by atom to create useful materials and devices (especially computers). Nanotechnology is already here. *Forbes* published Robert Paull, "The Top Ten Nanotech Products of 2003," which included high-performance ski wax and the world's first OLED digital camera. http://www.forbes.com/2003/12/29/cz_jw_1229soapbox.html (accessed July 7, 2007). General Motors uses nanoengineered material in the running boards of its SUVs and pickups.

102. Watts Wacker and Jim Taylor with Howard Means, *The Visionary's Handbook: Nine Paradoxes That Will Shape the Future of Your Business* (New York: HarperBusiness, 2000), 129.

103. Lawrence Lessig, "Insanely Destructive Devices: Trying to Defend Against Self-replicating Weapons of Mass Destruction," *Wired* (April 2004): 113,

http://www.wired.com/wired/archive/12.04/view.html?pg=5 (accessed January 25, 2005).

104. Thomas Friedman, *The World Is Flat: A Brief History of the Twenty-first Century* (New York: Farrar, Straus, Giroux, 2005).

105. Thomas Friedman, *The Lexus and the Olive Tree*, rev. ed. (New York: Farrar Straus Giroux, 2000), xx, ix. Globalization is defined as "a dynamic ongoing process" involving "the inexorable integration of markets, nation-states and technologies to a degree never witnessed before" (8). Here is a negative definition of globalization: "Globalization has produced a world economic system and trade laws that protect transnational corporations at the expense of human life, biodiversity, and the environment." See Steven Best and Douglas Kellner, *The Postmodern Adventure: Science, Technology, and Cultural Studies at the Third Millennium* (New York: Guildford Press, 2001), 1.

106. Van Wishard, "Understanding Our Moment in History: Living Between Two Ages," *Vital Speeches of the Day*, 71 (May 1, 2005): 443.

107. See Krysia Diver, "Cartoonist Faces Greek Jail for Blasphemy," *The Guardian* (March 23, 2005) http://arts.guardian.co.uk/news/story/0,11711,1443908,00.html (accessed April 29, 2006). Gerhard Haderer, *Das Leben des Jesus* (Vienna: Carl Ueberreuter, 2002).

108. A thousand-signature petition of international artists, signed by people including the Nobel prize winner Elfriede Jelinek, was delivered to the European Union to protest his arrest in Greece. Haderer's appeal before an Athens appeals court took place on April 13, 2005. Calling the case "daft," the appeals court cleared the Austrian cartoonist of committing blasphemy by publishing a humorous take on the life of Christ, and allowed the book to be openly sold again. See Diver, "Cartoonist Faces Greek Jail for Blasphemy," *The Guardian*. See also South East Europe Media Organization, "World Press Freedom Review 2005: Greece," *International Press Institute*, http://service.cms.apa.at/cms/ipi/freedom_detail-new.html?country=/KW0001/KW0003/KW0063/ (accessed May 10, 2006).

109. Words of Teilhard de Chardin just before he died, as quoted in Andrew Harvey, *The Way of Passion: A Celebration of Rumi* (Berkeley, Calif.: Frog, 1994), 3.

110. A Pearl Harbor illustration begins Thomas de Zengotita's book *Mediated: How the Media Shapes Your World and the Way You Live In It* (New York: Bloomsbury, 2005), 1.

111. Thomas de Zengotita describes how those who were present at Pearl Harbor on December 7 had personal stories that they could share. "Such stories are primal, anthropologically grounded." Those who read newspapers or listened to the radio for news about Pearl Harbor didn't experience the events in the same way—it didn't happen to them—and, therefore, they had no personal stories to tell.

According to Zengotita, the 1950s' television show *You Are There* was the "original miracle of television," because, for the first time, viewers became both eyewitnesses and participants to past and present world events. It was through television in real time that viewers experienced the assassination of President Kennedy and could later tell stories as if they were there. In the author's words, "you were there from so many different perspectives. You weren't in one spot, the way you would have been if you were physically there. . . . You had a sort of God's eye view." This personal perspective is a "form of flattery so pervasive," that it can account for the narcissism of our present age. "The flattered self is a mediated self, and . . . the osmotic process through which reality and representation fuse, gets carried into our psyches by the irresistible flattery that goes with being incessantly addressed."

Today's mediation possibilities far outshine those of the French royalty at Versailles, where the landscaping and architecture were designed to provide the king with vistas "that made it seem as if the whole world were spread out before him." Zengotita concludes: "that's peanuts compared to what mediation makes possible for all of us today." Thomas de Zengotita, *Mediated: How the Media Shapes Your World and the Way You Live in It* (New York: Bloomsbury, 2005), 6-8.

112. De Zengotita, *Mediated: How the Media Shapes Your World and the Way You Live in It*, 11.

113. Ibid., 5.

114. Wright, *A Short History of Progress*, 128.

115. For more on this, and how the bombings in Madrid and London were sparked less by Middle Eastern unease and more by European disaffections, see Ian Buruma, *Murder in Amsterdam: The Death of Theo van Gogh and the Limits of Tolerance* (New York: Penguin, 2006).

116. Wright, *A Short History of Progress*, 124-25.

117. Margot Roosevelt, "Evangelicals Go Green," *Time* (February 8, 2006), http://www.time.com/time/nation/article/0,8599,1157612,00.html (accessed July 4, 2007).

118. "National News Briefs: Orthodox Church Leader Declares Pollution a Sin," *New York Times* (November 10, 1997), http://query.nytimes.com/gst/fullpage.html?res=980DE1D61339F933A25752C1A961958260&n=Top%2fReference%2fTimes%20Topics%2fSubjects%2fR%2fReligion%20and%20Belief (accessed October 17, 2007).

119. Quoted by John Naisbitt, *Global Paradox: The Bigger the World Economy, the More Powerful Its Smallest Players* (New York: William Morrow, 1994), 19. Also quoted by Gerald A. Johnston, as reported in "Cooperation, Competition God Hand in Hand: Go-It-Alone Approach No Longer Viable in Interdependent World," *Nikkei Weekly—*Japan (May 13, 1993): 7.

120. In the next twenty years, the number of people sharing the water supply will reach nine billion. Only 2 percent of the world's store of water is potable or pure enough to be used for industries that need clean water. For the 2003 report of the United Nations Environment Programme, "Vital Water Graphics" An Overview of the State of the World's Fresh and Marine Waters," www.unep.org/vitalwater/index.htm (accessed January 19, 2005).

121. A first-quarter 2003 United Nations report predicts this. Today more than one billion people have limited access to clean water. For an example of the problem see the United Nations publication: "Population and Development Report: Water Scarcity in the Arab World," June 2004. For the general problem of water scarcity see "Freshwater: UNEP.Net, The Environment Network, http://freshwater.unep.net/index.cfm?

issue=water_scarcity (accessed January 19, 2005). By the way, the Colorado and the Rio Grande rivers in the United States and the Yellow River in China don't reach the sea anymore.

122. You need five liters for drinking, twenty for sanitation and hygiene, fifteen for bathing, and ten for preparing food. People in thirteen countries, nine of them in Africa, must try to live on an average of less than ten liters per day. For more see Paul Brown, "Failure to Manage Water Kills Two Million a Year—UN," *The Guardian* (April 12, 2002), http://www.guardian.co.uk/international/story/0,,682953,00.html (accessed January 24, 2005).

123. Quoted in Séan McDonagh, "The Water of Life," *Spirituality* 9 (January–February 2003): 49. See also his "The Cyril Hally Lecture: The Water of Life," 3, http://www.catholicearthcareoz.net/pdf/112002cyril_hallylecture.pdf (accessed May 10, 2006).

124. There are 3.79 liters per gallon, so $50 per liter equals $189.50 per gallon.

125. Referenced in Richard Shelton's review of *The Ocean at Home: An Illustrated History of the Aquarium* by Bernd Brunner (New York: Princeton Architectural Press, 2005), *TLS: Times Literary Supplement* (November 18, 2005): 28.

126. Paul Ehrlich, David Dobkin, and Daryl Wheye, *The Bird Watchers Handbook: A Guide to the Natural History of the Birds of Britain and Europe* (New York: Oxford University Press, 1994), 23.

127. "Today's environments depend on the earth's ice caps. Because the polar seas are cold, they are rich in oxygen and therefore teem with life. Cold meltwater from the polar ice streams across the ocean floors, bringing oxygen and abundant life to the abyss—and keeping vast amounts of hydrated methane locked up in the chilly abyssal mud. . . . Warmer and more stagnant, the seas then carry less oxygen, circulate fewer nutrients, and sustain less life." Matt Cartmill, "History of Science, *TLS: Times Literary Supplement* (September 9, 2005): 26. For more, see Tony Hallam, *Catastrophies and Lesser Calamites: The Causes of Mass Extinction* (New York: Oxford University Press, 2004).

128. So says the World Health Organization.

129. Wendell Berry, "Quality vs. Form," *The Way of Ignorance and Other Essays* (Emeryville, Calif.: Shoemaker & Hoard, 2005), 86.

130. Wright, *A Short History of Progress*, 131.

131. Edward Echlin, "We're All Responsible for the Earth," *The Tablet* (April 1, 2006): 25.

132. John James Audubon in his essay, "My Style of Drawing Birds," *Writings and Drawings*, ed. Christoph Irmscher (New York: Library of America, 1999), 761. Thanks to Amy Newman, "Wondering Thomas," *Image: Art, Faith, Mystery*, 48 (Winter 2005/06): 106, for pointing me to this account.

133. Emily Dickinson, "Split the Lark—and You'll Find the Music," *The Complete Poems of Emily Dickinson, ed. Thomas H. Johnson* (Boston: Little, Brown, 1960) 412. Also quoted in Amy Newman, "Wondering Thomas," *Image: Art, Faith, Mystery*, 48 (Winter 2005/06), 106.

134. *The New York Times* did a front-page article on how the medical establishment,

in partnership with the insurance industry, is in a place where bad health is good business. The example they used was diabetics: it is more profitable to amputate limbs and treat the complications from diabetes, than to provide preventative care for people with diabetes so that they don't have to get their limbs taken off . . . or die. "Insurers, for example, will often refuse to pay $150 for a diabetic to see a podiatrist, who can help prevent foot ailments associated with the disease. Nearly all of them, though, cover amputations which typically cost more than $30,000." Ian Urbina, "In the Treatment of Diabetes, Success Often Does Not Pay," *New York Times* (January 11, 2006): 1.

## 2. Man Overboard!

1. Mark 4:35-41.

2. Cf. "Surviving a Storm at Sea," Boating Resource Center [resource online]; available at http://www.boatingmadesimple.com/storm.htm (accessed June 30, 2006).

3. See John Rousmaniere, *Fastnet, Force 10* (New York: W.W. Norton & Co., 1980, 2000).

4. See Rob Mundle, *Fatal Storm—The Inside Story of the Tragic Sydney-Hobart Race* (Blacklick, Ohio: McGraw-Hill, 2000) and G. Bruce Knecht, *The Proving Ground* (Boston: Little, Brown & Co., 2001).

5. Extensive information on Jordan's series drogue is available on his website: http://www.jordanseriesdrogue.com (accessed July 6, 2007). Additional information is available from Carey Deringer, "Drag Devices: Sea Anchors and Drogues," in *Good Old Boat* (Jan/Feb 2002), published online at http://www.sea-anchors.com/goodold boat.htm (accessed July 6, 2007). The U.S. Coast Guard test results for Jordan's series drogue are available at http://seriesdrogue.com/coastguardreport (accessed July 6, 2007).

6. The ingenuity of the series drogue lies in the fact that the cones (drag devices) are located all along the length of the rope. Therefore, if half the cones are inactive within the slack portion of a wave, the other half are still capable of creating a drag on the boat. Also, if a large wave is approaching from an angle off the stern, the drag devices closest to the boat (where rope elasticity is low) will create a load much faster than if a large, single drogue attached to the line. Also, the chain at the end of the rope keeps the drogue below the waves, which helps maintain constant tension on the rope and consistent drag on the boat.

7. See Jordan's website, cited above.

8. Luke 14:27-33.

9. 1 John 4:18.

10. *Agape* is used infrequently in Greek literature prior to the writings of the New Testament, but acquires extraordinary depth and significance in the sayings and writings of Jesus and the apostles.

11. John 3:16.

12. Eph 5:2.

13. Gal 2:19.

14. Gal 5:24.

15. Gal 5:19-21.

16. 1 Cor 15:31 ASV.
17. See Rom 6:6; Eph 4:22; Col 3:9 ASV.
18. 1 Cor 15:20.
19. Mark 8:34; see also Matt 10:38; 16:24 and Luke 9:23; 14:27.
20. Rom 8:29.
21. Col 3:3, 4; see also Matt 10:39; 16:25; Mark 8:35; Luke 9:24; 17:33; John 12:25.
22. Phil 3:21.
23. Phil 1:6; Col 1:24.
24. Samuel Taylor Coleridge, "The Rime of the Ancient Mariner," *The Poetical Works of S. T. Coleridge, with Memoir, Notes, etc.* (New York: Thomas Y. Crowell, 1890), 117.

### 3. In Sync with Jesus and the First Perfect Stormers

1. Danah Zohar and Ian Marshall, *Spiritual Capital: Wealth We Can Live By* (London: Bloomsbury Press, 2004), 68-70.
2. Fortunately, we are not at the mercy of those neural connections in our heads. Put differently, faith cannot be reduced to this God-spot in our brains. The inherited genetic pool in which we all swim is a given, but our biological hardware does not make us victims of neurological determinism. Gareth Jones sums it up well when he says: "What I am as a person cannot be reduced to what my brain is." "A Neurobiological Portrait of the Human Person: Finding a Context for Approaching the Brain," in Joel B. Green, ed., *What about the Soul? Neuroscience and Christian Anthropology* (Nashville: Abingdon Press, 2004), 31-46.
3. Aristotle, *Politics: A Treatise on Government* (London: George Routledge and Sons, 1895).
4. Marcus Porcius Cato and Marcus Terentius Varro, *On Agriculture*, rev. ed. trans. W. D. Hooper and H. B. Ash (Cambridge, Mass.: Harvard University Press, 1979).
5. Bruce J. Malina. *The New Testament World: Insights from Cultural Anthropology*, rev. ed. (Louisville: Westminster John Knox Press, 2001), 36.
6. For more information on slavery, see T. Wiedeman, *Greek and Roman Slavery* (New York: Routledge, 1988); J. S. Jeffers, *The Greco-Roman World of the New Testament Era* (Downers Grove, Ill: InterVarsity Press, 1999), and Stephan Joubert, *Paul as Benefactor: Reciprocity, Strategy and Theological Reflection in Paul's Collection* (Tubingen: Mohr Siebeck, 2000).
7. K. C. Hanson and D. E. Oakman, *Palestine in the Time of Jesus: Social Structures and Social Conflicts* (Minneapolis: Fortress Press, 1998), 131-60.
8. Matt 8:3.
9. Matt 9:23-26; Luke 7:11-17.
10. Matt 9:20-22.
11. Luke 9:36-50.
12. Mark 7.
13. Matt 9:11; Luke 19:1-10.
14. John 4; Matt 15.
15. Matt 23:16-21.

16. John 4:21-23.
17. John 2:19-22.
18. See also the informative study by Joseph H. Hellerman, *The Ancient Church as Family* (Minneapolis: Fortress Press, 2001).
19. Matt 18:1-4; Luke 8:1-3.
20. 1 Cor 13.
21. 1 Thess 1:6
22. 1 Thess 1:8.
23. Acts 17.

## 4. Seasoned Sailors

1. *Wahine*, pronounced "wah-hee-nay," is a New Zealand Maori word meaning *woman*.
2. No warning or weather report had been unheard or unheeded. The ship was well equipped, and the crew was well prepared. They had practiced lifeboat drills, checked the lifeboat motors and lowering procedures.
3. The lights of Baring heads (to the west) and Pencarrow heads (to the east).
4. On land, a seven-year-old girl was killed as she lay in her bed when sheets of roofing iron blew through her bedroom window. Others died that day; many more were left injured and homeless. Fifty-one of those on board the *Wahine* also lost their lives.
5. Max Lambert and Jim Hartley, *The Wahine Disaster* (Wellington, New Zealand: A. H. & A. W. Reed, 1969), 41.
6. Lambert and Hartley, *The Wahine Disaster*, 42.
7. Ibid., 45.
8. Definition drawn from *The Oxford English Dictionary*.
9. For example, see Eugene Peterson, *Working the Angles: The Shape of Pastoral Integrity* (Grand Rapids, Mich.: Eerdmans, 1987).
10. For example, we have given up delving into the depths of theological thought and becoming immersed in the wisdom of the great leaders of faith from previous centuries.
11. Put another way, they want to move beyond the safe playpens and nurseries of faith they have found in the church. Or, to continue our metaphor, they have become dissatisfied with always rowing a small boat or sailing within the harbor's secure waters.
12. Here they can explore the rawer, deeper, and less safe places of Christian faith and real life. Their journeys of faith are like solo sailing into the deeper, richer, and scarier places of God.
13. Captain Robertson had been at sea for nearly forty years before this storm tested his seamanship to the extreme. He had weathered many storms, survived at least one previous shipwreck, studied, read, and practiced his craft for decades.
14. Mike Riddell, *Godzone: A Traveller's Guide* (Oxford: Lion Publishing, 1992), 43.
15. It was Teilhard de Chardin who said, "In all those dark moments, O God grant that I may understand that it is you who are painfully parting the fibres of my being in order to penetrate to the very marrow of my substance." Pierre Teilhard de Chardin, *The Divine Milieu: An Essay on the Interior Life* (New York: Harper, 1960), 62.

16. See "Saint Brendan's Prayer," http://www.saintbrendans-cec.org/StBrendan.dsp (accessed July 4, 2007).

17. These imaginings were borrowed, with permission, from Mark Berry's "St. Brendan Meditation," http://markjberry.blogs.com/way_out_west/2006/03/index.html (accessed July 9, 2007).

18. See Sir Francis Drake's prayer, http://www.worldprayers.org/frameit.cgi?/archive/prayers/invocations/disturb_us_lord_when_we.html (accessed July 4, 2007).

## 5. Exposing Our Murky Motives

1. 1 Cor 13:13 TNIV.
2. Christian Smith, "Church Without Clergy," http://awildernessvoice.com/ChurchWithoutClergy.html (accessed July 4, 2007).
3. Exod 18:14 *"THE MESSAGE."*
4. Exod 18:15-16 *"THE MESSAGE."*
5. Exod 18:17-23 *"THE MESSAGE."*
6. Num 11:16-17 *"THE MESSAGE."*
7. Num 11:24-25 *"THE MESSAGE."*
8. Num 11:26 *"THE MESSAGE."*
9. Num 11:27-28 *"THE MESSAGE."*
10. Num 11:29 *"THE MESSAGE."*
11. Eph 4:12.
12. John 13:1-5 *"THE MESSAGE."*
13. John 13:1 *"THE MESSAGE."*
14. John 13:3 *"THE MESSAGE."*

## 6. Reorienting the Church of the Twenty-first Century

1. For more see Leonard Sweet, *Out of the Question . . . Into the Mystery: Getting Lost in the GodLife Mystery* (Colorado Springs: Waterbrook Press, 2004), 8-10.
2. John Elya, "May They Be One: When the Two Strong Men Meet," http://elyastrongmen.notlong.com (accessed April 5, 2006).
3. Such a simplification of Korean church history may be problematic for some church historians. Yet the purpose of this article is simply to identify the major forces in the development of Korean church ministry.
4. Matt 28:18-20.
5. In fact, this spiritual awakening had been a result of "Revival Movement in Wonsan, 1903" led by a Methodist missionary, Robert A. Hardie.
6. Kyunghyang Shinmun, (19 January 2006).
7. Mark 1:35 TNIV.
8. Luke 6:12 TNIV.
9. Patricia D. Brown, *Path to Prayer: Finding Your Own Way to the Presence of God* (San Fransico: Jossey-Bass, 2003). See also "Tongsung Kido (Pray Aloud), *United Methodist Book of Worship* (Nashville: The United Methodist Publishing House, 1992), #446.

10. Byoungho Zoh, *Bible Tongdok and Intuition*, Korean ed. (Seoul: Tangessungulssi, 2004), 17-18.

11. 2 Tim 3:16-17 TNIV.

12. *Saebyuk Gidohoe*, along with Chulya Gidohoe, always comes with *Tongsung Gido* and Bible *Tongdok*.

13. Kukminilbo, 25 (February, 2006): 21.

14. Leonard Sweet, Brian D. McLaren, and Jerry Haselmayer, *A is for Abductive: The Language of the Emerging Church* (Grand Rapids, Mich.: Zondervan, 2003), 145. See also Arthur Koestler, *Janus* (London: Hutchinson, 1978), 57.

15. Sweet, McLaren, and Haselmayer, *A is for Abductive: The Language of the Emerging Church*, 145.

16. George Santayana, "Intuitive Morality," in *Little Essays Drawn from the Writings of George Santayana*, ed. Logan Pearsall Smith (New York: Charles Scribner's Sons, 1921), 237.

17. A popular variant of "Two sorts of truth: trivialities, where opposites are obviously absurd, and profound truths, recognized by the fact that the opposite is also a profound truth." Quoted in Hans Bohr, "My Father," *Neils Bohr: His Life and Work as Seen by his Friends and Colleagues* (Baltimore: Johns Hopkins University Press, 1967), 328.

18. G. K. Chesterton, *Orthodoxy* (New York: John Lane, 1912), 47.

19. John 12:24-25 TNIV.

20. Holt A. Clarke, *Created For God's Mission: Fashioning a Great Commission Church for a 21st Century World* (Bloomington, Ind.: Authorhouse, 2006): 215-19.

21. This church-planting mission has been carried out covertly to protect the missionaries and their work.

22. The similar case can be found in the Church Multiplication ministry of NorthWood Church, Texas. (Pastor, Bob Roberts, Jr.). According to the church webpage, "Since 1992, NorthWood Church Multiplication Center has started almost 90 churches. . . . We now have clusters of our churches in 19 cities throughout the United States. Sixty-two new churches have been planted in the network in 2005" (http://www.northwoodchurch.org/v2/glocal.htm [accessed June 12, 2007]).

23. "Missional living." *Wikipedia*, http://en.wikipedia.org/wiki/Missional_living (accessed June 12, 2007). See also Chris Seay, "Is Pomo Nomo? A Postmodern Pastor Reaches Out to the Mod Squad," LeadershipJournal.net, 20 February 2003), http://www.christianitytoday.com/leaders/newsletter/2003/cln30220.html (accessed June 12, 2007).

24. *The United Christian Newspaper*, 19 June 2005.

25. Acts 1:4, 8 TNIV.

26. Matt 28:19-20 TNIV.

## 7. The Perfect Storm as a Paradigmic Theory

1. 1 Cor 1:22-23 NIV.

2. Heb 11:1.

3. Matt 26:26.

## 9. The Tides Are Turning

1. J. R. R. Tolkien, “The White Rider,” bk. 3, ch. 5 of *The Two Towers*, being pt. 2 of *The Lord of the Rings*, 2d ed. (Boston: Houghton Mifflin, 1965), 98.

2. The turning of the tide is literally the change of the tide from incoming to outgoing, or vice versa.

3. *Perfection*, as it is understood in the Sermon on the Mount (“Be perfect, as your heavenly Father is perfect.” Matthew 5:48), means “completeness” or “wholeness.”

4. St. Irenaeus, second-century Bishop of Lyons writes, “The glory of God is man fully alive” (*Against Heresies*, bk. 4, ch. 20.7). St. Athanasius writes, “God became man so that man might become God” (*The Incarnation*).

5. See http://www.weather.com/aboutus/television/ocms/cantore.html?from=tv_personality (accessed April 3, 2007).

6. Mark 15:13.

7. Matt 27:25.

8. See Richard Dawkins, *The God Delusion* (Boston: Houghton Mifflin, 2006) and Sam Harris, *Letter to a Christian Nation* (New York: Alfred A. Knopf, 2007) for a taste of the new atheism.

9. See Isa 27:1.

10. Job 9:8.

11. Read Numbers 22:21-39. I have a hard time not hearing the voice of Eddie Murphy as the donkey now that I’ve seen the *Shrek* movies.

12. 1 Kgs 19:10-15.

13. 1 Kgs 19:12 NKJV.

14. Rev 1:15 TNIV.

15. *The Book of Common Prayer and Administration of the Sacraments and the Ceremonies of the Church, Together with the Psalter of Psalms of David, According to the Episcopal Church* (New York: Oxford University Press, 1990), 298.

16. I think Thomas Merton first coined the phrase “body of broken bones” in a chapter called “A Body of Broken Bones” of his book *Seeds of Contemplation* (Norfolk, Conn.: New Directions, 1949), 53-58.

17. In some churches, salt is still added to the baptismal waters. When I begin a new round of formation courses, part of the first class is sprinkling salt on the tongues of those gathered.

18. A sermon has three points; a homily has one point. A homilette has no point whatsoever. My friend Len Sweet says that in this postmodern era, the best sermons are “pointless.” They don’t make points; they encourage experiences.

19. We don’t gather, but we *are gathered* by the Holy Spirit for worship. Thanks to the Reverend Dr. Ralph McMichael for this insight.

20. See Acts 2:14-40.

21. Acts 5:12-16.

22. Lord Jesus, stay with us, for evening is at hand and the day
is past; be our companion in the way, kindle our hearts, and
awaken hope, that we may know you as you are revealed in

Scripture and the breaking of bread. Grant this for the sake of your love. Amen.

"A Collect for the Presence of Christ," *The Book of Common Prayer and Administration of the Sacraments and the Ceremonies of the Church, Together with the Psalter of Psalms of David, According to the Episcopal Church* (New York: Oxford University Press, 1990), 124.

23. Being "Christ*like*" doesn't cut it. I'm advocating the ancient Orthodox understanding of theosis here. Paul reflects this when he says, "For me, to live is Christ and to die is gain" (Phil 1:21).

24. *Anglican Communion News Service* #4272, http://www.anglicancommunion.org/acns/articles/42/50/acns4272.cfm (accessed April 12, 2007).

25. C. S. Lewis, *The Lion, the Witch and the Wardrobe* (New York: Macmillan Publishing, 1970), 75-76.

26. 2 Cor 5:17 AT.

27. Leonard Sweet said this in his *The Jesus Prescription for a Healthy Life* (Nashville: Abingdon Press, 1996), 113, where he quotes from Wendell Berry, *Sex, Economy, Freedom & Community: Eight Essays* (New York: Pantheon Books, 1993), xiv.

28. John 3:16.

29. Rom 5:8.

30. *The Book of Common Prayer and Administration of the Sacraments and the Ceremonies of the Church, Together with the Psalter of Psalms of David, According to the Episcopal Church* (New York: Oxford University Press, 1990), 101.

## 10. The Relationships of Winds and Waves

1. George McLeod, *Only One Way Left* (Glasgow: The Iona Community, 1956), 38.

2. See Acts 17:16-34.

3. Martin Lindstrom, *Brand Sense: How to Build Powerful Brands through Touch, Taste, Smell, Sight and Sound* (New York: Free Press, 2005) 172.

4. Andrew Fletcher, *The Political Works of Andrew Fletcher, Esq.* (London: A. Bettesworth and C. Hatch and J. Clarke, 1732), 372.

5. Bob Briner, *Roaring Lambs: A Gentle Plan to Radically Change Our World* (Grand Rapids, Mich.: Zondervan, 1993), 177.

6. Ibid., 31.

## 11. Between Spirit and Culture

1. This phrase was coined by Wilberforce in 1787 and quoted in Eric Metaxas, *Amazing Grace: William Wilberforce and the Heroic Campaign to End Slavery* (San Francisco: HarperSanFrancisco, 2007), 85.

2. For further insight, see my book *Road Runner* (Nashville: Abingdon Press, 2002).

3. My paraphrase of Micah 7:1-7.

4. For further insight, see also my book *Talisman: Global Positioning for the Soul* (St. Louis: Chalice Press, 2006).

5. For further, more individualized and Christian, perspective, see also my book

*Christian OptiMystics: Riding the Rapids of Spirit*, co-authored with Dwayne Ratzlaff (St. Louis: Chalice Press, 2006).

6. See also my book *Why Should I Believe You?* (Nashville: Abingdon Press, 2006).

7. Paul Tillich, "Storms of Our Times," *The Protestant Era*, trans. James Luther Adams (Chicago: University of Chicago Press, 1948), 237-52.

8. Ibid., 248.

9. "But what I do know is that if the meaning of this war is not understood and accepted, night will fall over us for generations." Tillich, "Storms of Our Times," *The Protestant Era*, 252.

## 12. Celestial Storms: Dreaming of Novae

1. Gen 7:11 NIV.
2. Jonah 1:12.
3. Matt 5:3-10 NIV.
4. Matt 16:25.
5. Rev 22:16-17.

## 13. Manual and Chart Notes for Stormy Seas

1. Thanks to David Laubach for pointing me to this biblical text.

2. Anthony C. Thiselton, *The First Epistle to the Corinthians: A Commentary on the Greek Text* (Grand Rapids, Mich.: Eerdmans, 2000), 1022.

3. William Arthur Ward, "To Risk." http//www.appleseeds.org/to-risk_WAW/htm (accessed October 20, 2007).

4. Emily Dickinson, "[Letter] to Abiah Root, late 1850," *The Letters of Emily Dickinson*, ed. Thomas H. Johnson (Cambridge, Mass.: Belknap Press of Harvard University Press, 1958), 1:104 [letter 39].

5. In the "Apostolic Letter *Novo Millennio Ineunte* of his Holiness Pope John Paul II to the Bishops, Clergy, and Lay Faithful at the Close of the Great Jubilee of the Year 2000," Pope John Paul II admonished the church to "Put out into the deep" (http://www.vatican.va/holy_father/john_paul_ii/apost_letters/documents/hf_jp ii_apl_20010106_novo-millennio-ineunte_en.html [accessed June 29, 2006]).

6. For example, Islamic fundamentalists see Western forms of modernization and predict the extinction of Islam as we know it.

7. Redmond O'Hanlon, *Trawler* (New York: Alfred A. Knopf, 2005), 9.

8. David Dunkle, "'Painter of Light' Offers Warm and Welcoming Images," *Texas Baptist Standard*, 14 November 2005, 11. http://www.baptiststandard.com/postnuke/index.php?module=htmlpages&func=display&pid=4181 (accessed May 29, 2006). A 15-by-22 foot Kinkade country village scene owned by a private collector in Pennsylvania cost one million dollars, and another $120,000 to install. "Kinkade envy: Status symbol emerges as paintings grow massive," LarkNews.com 3 (29 May 2006), http://www.larknews.com/december_2005/secondary.php?page=1 (accessed May 29, 2006).

9. Samuel Hazo, "Poets and Poetry: The Autobiographers of Everybody," *Vital Speeches of the Day* 71 (15 January 2005), 220-21.

10. John 20:20.

11. Two huge billboards found on I-35 between San Marcos and New Braunfels (Texas) make this claim. Thanks to Landrum Leavell III for this reference.

12. John Wesley, "Now I Have Found the Ground Wherein," *A Collection of Hymns for the Use of the Methodist Episcopal Church Principally from the Collection of the Rev. John Wesley, rev. and corrected, with a Supplement* (Cincinnati: Published by J. F. Wright and L. Swormstedt, 1844), 343-44.

13. Thanks to Pastor David Schultz for this image.

14. Emily Dickinson, "Exultation Is the Going," *The Complete Poems of Emily Dickinson*, ed. Thomas H. Johnson (Boston: Little, Brown, 1960), 39-40.

15. Attributed to Mark Twain, but not considered authentic, according to "Mark Twain Quotations - Discovery," <http://www.twainquotes.com/Discovery.html>. (Accessed 28 December 2005)

16. This fourteenth stanza of "Amazing Grace" was added after the original six verses were published in the *Olney Hymns* in 1779 and is not necessarily by John Newton. Compare it with second stanza of Isaac Watts, "Am I A Soldier of the Cross?" *The United Methodist Hymnal: Book of United Methodist Worship* (Nashville: The United Methodist Publishing House, 1989), 511. For more information, see "Glasgow Guide," http://www.glasgowguide.co.uk/wjmc/amazingg.shtml (accessed October 20, 2007).

17. "Buffalo," http://stonyfordranch.com/buffalo.html (accessed 17 March 2006).

18. I borrow this powerful metaphor from John Taylor's *The Go-Between God: The Holy Spirit and the Christian Mission* (Philadelphia: Fortress Press, 1973).

19. This point is made more eloquently by British theologian John Taylor, *The Go-Between God: The Holy Spirit and the Christian Mission* (Philadelphia: Fortress Press, 1973), 177-78: "At the end of the day it is not our following of him that gives us any value but his hold on us."

20. Albert B. Simpson (1843–1919), "Launch Out," in *Hymns of the Christian Life: A Book of Worship in Song Emphasizing Evangelism, Missions, and the Deeper Life*, rev. and enl. ed. (Harrisburg, Pa.: Christian Publications, 1962), 242.

21. Alain De Botton, *The Art of Travel* (New York: Pantheon, 2002), 148.

22. Acts 27:18 calls the storm an *eujrakuvlwn* (NAS—*Euraquilo*, ASV—*Euraclydon*, TNIV—*Northeaster*). Thanks to Alan Ehlers for pointing out this similarity between Paul's shipwreck and the *Andrea Gail* story.

23. See Acts 27:18, 19.

24. *Oxford English Dictionary*, 2d ed., ed. J. A. Simpson and E. S. C. Weiner (Oxford: Clarendon Press, 1989), 13:479.

25. The Latin is: *In necessasariis, unitas; In dubiis, libertas; in omnibus, caritas.* The quote is reportedly found in *Imitation of Christ* (bk. I, ch. III), *Of the Imitation of Christ*, tr. from the Latin original ascribed to Thomas à Kempis, by T. F. Dibdin (London: Pickering, 1851).

26. John Wilkie, "Under My Feet," *Sprout 'N Shout: Songs for All God's Children*, produced by Richard Wilson (Charlotte: Sprout 'N Shout Ministries, 1996) http://www.sproutnshout.com/undermyfeet.html (accessed December 16, 2006). Used by permission.

27. For the early church's identification of the cross with the mast, see the mar-

velous chapter on "The Sea" in Peter Dronke's *Imagination in the Late Pagan and Early Christian World: The First Nine Centuries A.D.* (Florence, Italy: SISMEL, Edizioni del Galluzzo, 2003), 69-100. Dronke quotes Ambrose in the fourth book of his *Commentary on St. Luke*, where he compared the Homeric sailor with the Christian one: "It is not a matter of shutting one's ears [to the Sirens], but of opening them so that Christ's voice can be heard: no one who listens to it will be afraid of shipwreck; he does not have to be tied to the mast-tree like Ulysses by physical chains, but his mind must be bound to the tree of the cross by the spirit's fetters" (78).

28. From the refrain of George Bennard's 1913 hymn, "The Old Rugged Cross," *Hymns of Praise, Numbers One and Two Combined: For the Church and Sunday School*, comp. F. G. Kingsbury (Chicago: Hope Publishing, 1926), 27.

29. See Matt 14.

30. Albert Johnston was on another sword boat east of the *Andrea Gail* during the Perfect Storm of 1991. He gave this account of the experience: "We went into it until it started to get dark, and then we turned around and went with it. You can't see those rogue waves in the dark and you don't want to get blasted and knock your wheelhouse off. We got the RPM tuned in just right to be in synch with the waves; too fast and we'd start surfing, too slow and the waves would blast right over the whole boat. The boat was heavy and loaded with fish, very stable. It made for an amazingly good ride." Sebastian Junger, *The Perfect Storm: A True Story of Men Against the Sea* (New York: Norton, 1997), 118.

31. Mark 4:35-41.

32. Rom 8:39 TNIV.

33. Phil 1:21 TNIV.

34. 2 Cor 5:8 TNIV.

35. John Newton, Letter VIII, 19 January 1763, *The Works of the Rev. John Newton . . . To Which Are Prefixed, Memoirs of His Life, Etc.* by Richard Cecil (New York: Robert Carter, 1844), 1:98.

36. Phillips Brooks, "O Little Town of Bethlehem," 1867.

37. Dawna Markova, *I Will Not Die an Unlived Life: Reclaiming Purpose and Passion* (Berkeley, Calif.: Conari Press, 2000), 1.